LEEDS

Edited by Donna Samworth

First published in Great Britain in 2003 by
YOUNG WRITERS
Remus House,
Coltsfoot Drive,
Peterborough, PE2 9JX
Telephone (01733) 890066

Copyright Contributors 2003

SB ISBN 1 84460 247 8

FOREWORD

Young Writers was established in 1991 as a foundation for promoting the reading and writing of poetry amongst children and young adults. Today it continues this quest and proceeds to nurture and guide the writing talents of today's youth.

From this year's competition Young Writers is proud to present a showcase of the best poetic talent from across the UK. Each hand-picked poem has been carefully chosen from over 66,000 'Hullabaloo!' entries to be published in this, our eleventh primary school series.

This year in particular we have been wholeheartedly impressed with the quality of entries received. The thought, effort, imagination and hard work put into each poem impressed us all and once again the task of editing was a difficult but enjoyable experience.

We hope you are as pleased as we are with the final selection and that you and your family will continue to be entertained with *Hullabaloo! Leeds* for many years to come.

CONTENTS

Jordan Walker (10)   15
Luke Muffitt (10)   15
Eugene Falconer (11)   16
Samuel Richardson (11)   16
Angelica Sykes (10)   17
George Grant (10)   17
Daniel Waite (10)   18
Carl Rushforth (11)   18
Sian McMullan (11)   19

Bramley St Peter's CE Primary School

Jack Gillespie (9)   19
Matthew Johnson (9)   20
Lauren Hutchinson (10)   20
Danielle Pinkney (10)   21
Dane Hiscocks (9)   21
Sapphire Walker (10)   22
Devon Coates (10)   23
Loutia Kay (10)   23
Amy Walker (10)   24
Samantha Dennis-Bartle (9)   24
Ryan Wilson (10)   24
Stephanie Marston (9)   25
Jake Webber (10)   25
Abigail Cliff (10)   26
Kailey Jane Edwards (9)   26
Michael Hunter (10)   27
Michael Ash (9)   27
Laken Scholey (10)   28
Sheridan Mackey (9)   28
Kirsten McGann (9)   29
Chelsea Wood (9)   29
Jade Dixon (10)   30
Natasha Scott (9)   30
Ryan Scott (9)   31
Faye Haseltine (10)   31

Burton Salmon CP School

Holly Walton (9)	32
Joe Gardner (11)	32
Jessica Hunter (11)	33

Horsforth St Margaret's CE Primary School

Lauren Watson (9)	33
Brett Fisher (8)	34
Philip Hickman (9)	34
Daniel Greenway (9)	35
Jordan Richmond (9)	35
Charlotte Green (9)	36
Billy Simpson (9)	36
Lois Brown (8)	37
Jonathan Bargh (9)	37
Lucinda Layfield (9)	38
Alice Perfettini (8)	38
Lewis Naiff (8)	39
Luke Jowsey (9)	39
William Caress (9)	40
Abigail Grant (9)	40
Lucy Stephens (8)	41
Hannah Barker (8)	41
Alice Pickering (8)	42
Joe Carroll (8)	42
Amy Dobson (8)	43
Emily Woodgate (8)	43
Naomi Milton (8)	44
Jack Baker (9)	45
Matthew Evans (8)	45
Rebecca Cantlow (9)	46
Chelsea Birdsall (9)	46
Isobel Ridsdale (8)	47
Jessica Russell (8)	48
Helen Wilson (8)	48
Emma Jeffries (9)	49
Rosie Baker (9)	49
Jessica Womack (8)	50

Oliver Calimer (9)	50
James Bell (11)	51
Sara Pickering (8)	51
Kirsty Toomes (10)	52
Emily Hall (9)	52
Naomi Metcalfe (9)	53
Jacob Womack (10)	53
Mark Rawlinson (9)	54
Matangi Patel (9)	54
Sanderson Lam (9)	55
Joshua Falcon (8)	55
Maria Cullingworth (9)	56
Amy Sheard (9)	56
Matthew Shaw (8)	57
Chazz McHale (8)	57
Hannah Dobson (11)	58
Samuel Fairburn (8)	58
Anna Sandham (8)	59
Amy Foster (8)	59
Georgina Laws (10)	60
Sarah Northfield (9)	60
Matthew Barker (11)	61
Iona Griffiths (10)	61
Matthew Temple (10)	62
Josh O'Hara (10)	62
Natalie Fox (11)	63
Tom Jeffries (11)	63
Alex Crowther (11)	64
Alexander Hall (11)	64
Elise Johnson (11)	65
Simon Barker (11)	66
Andrew Pickering (11)	67
Ellie Singleton (11)	68

Kirkstall Valley Primary School

Yannek Bendler (10)	68
Nathan Hargreaves (10)	69
Letitia Archibald (11)	70

Daniel Robinson (10)	71
Hannah Leonard (10)	71
Charlotte Carrick (10)	72

Lawns Park Primary School

Charlotte Wainwright (8)	72
Ellecia McLoughlin (8)	73
Amy Florance Whitaker (8)	73
Sophie Dickson (8)	73
Amy Robinson (9)	74
Zoe Popple (9)	75
Kim Taylor (8)	75
Lucy Coultas (8)	76
Jack Shell (8)	76
Liberty Wightman (9)	77
Jamie McKue (9)	77
Georgia Dean (8)	78
Matthew Sorby (8)	78
Toni Bulger (10)	79
Thomas Southwell (7)	79
Katie Keeligan (9)	80

Leeds Grammar School

Alex Mavor (10)	80
Sam Barnett (11)	81
Tom Best (11)	82
Keiron Garrity (10)	82
Jamie Morris (11)	83
Robert Nicholson (10)	83
Peter Fisher (11)	84
Adam Bergen (10)	84
Sam Brown (10)	85
David Franklin (11)	86
James Shippey (11)	87
Alex Davidson (11)	87
Haydon Davidson (10)	88
Joe Watson (11)	89
Joe Wallen (11)	90

Rudy Harris (10)	91
Russell Heatley (10)	92
Thomas Papworth-Smith (10)	93
Jacob Francis Ehrlich (10)	94
Thomas Pettican (10)	95
Alex Watson (11)	95
Duncan Hallam (10)	96
Marco Sarussi (11)	96
Jonathan Letts (10)	97
Robert Morgan (11)	98
Luke Mirzabaigian (10)	99
Sam Grant (10)	100
William Lord (10)	101
Matthew McGoldrick (11)	102
Michael Ballmann (11)	103
James Leftley (11)	104
Fraser Dunlop (11)	105

Manston St James Primary School

Sean Longthorpe (10)	105
Jack Walker (11)	106
Bethany Pryor (10)	107
Joseph Kerry (11)	108
Matthew Wise (10)	109
Robyn Ward (11)	110
Courtney Parr (11)	110

Micklefield CE Primary School

Kayleigh Schietaert (9)	111
Kieran Martin-Rushworth (7)	111
Jessica Kidd (8)	112
Joshua Eyles (8)	112
Ashleigh Roberts (9)	113
Emma Stanley (8)	113
Elizabeth Grace (7)	114
Thomas McNally (7)	114
Lewis Parker (9)	115
Johnny Smith (9)	115

Haleema Nadir (10)   137
Bethany Wright (10)   137
Joe Ingham (10)   138
Jessica Kempner (10)   139
Oliver Packman (9)   140
Celia Helen Marker (9)   141
Oliver Dixon (10)   142
Ben Sweeting (9)   142
Charlie Fairbank (10)   143
William Harrison (8)   143
Edward Crocker (10)   144
Lauren Parkin (11)   144
Alex Smithies (11)   145
James Martin (11)   146
Sarah Milne (11)   147
Daniel Mercer (10)   148
Natalie Donkin (11)   149
Rebecca Jones (10)   150
Matthew Smith (11)   151
Joshua Habergham (11)   152
Wow, wow, wow!   153
Louise Naylor (10)   153
Wilf Mayson (11)   153
Molly Harper (8)   154
Lucy Worstenholme (8)   155
Rachel Zagajewski (11)   156
Tanis Isaac (9)   157
Sebastian Erkults (9)   158
Georgina Isle   159
Barnaby McMahon (10)   160

Rothwell CE I&J School

Hollie-Elise Kitchen (11)   161
Lucy Winterbottom (11)   162
Bethany Spencer (10)   163
Megan Elyse Burwell (10)   164
Ruth Cressall (11)   165
Dean Nuttall (11)   166

Rothwell Victoria Junior School

Stephanie Lawson (9)	166
Stacey Jefferson (9)	167
Rebecca Parker (9)	167
Connor Anthony Scott (9)	168
Jessica Ley (9)	168
Ashlea Cunningham (10)	169
Rebecca Kellegher (10)	170
Kirstie Backhouse (11)	170
Ellen Watson (10)	171
Gemma Wilson (11)	172
Claire Comer (10)	173
Jessica Murrell (9)	174
Aiden Packer (9)	175
Nina Harbour (11)	176
Laura Portrey (11)	177
Rosie Zanetti (10)	178
Rachel Kennedy (11)	179

Royal Park Primary School

Hennah Kiran (9)	179
Sanya Ikram (9)	180
Megan Parker (9)	180
Coran Sloss (10)	180
Carlo Corey (10)	181
Haleema Iqbal (11)	181
Kes Mansoor (11)	181
Adnan Ghafoor (9)	182
Libby Crane (8)	182
Donald Chitembwe (10)	182
Cameron Robinson (9)	183
Owen Corey (9)	183
Ayesha Shafiq Rehman (9)	184

St Matthew's CE Primary School

Thomas Eyles (10)	185
Tiffany Lawrence (10)	186
Jack Hallas (9)	186

Scott Haining (10)	186
Monica Rooprai (10)	187
Ben Jenkins (10)	187
Amy Sylvester (10)	187
Tom McFadyen (10)	188
Ajay Kumar (10)	188
Suraiya Bertie (10)	188
Rosemary Pollock (10)	189
Natalie Atherton (9)	189
Harry Crocker (9)	190
Josie Moulton (9)	190
Callum Armstrong (11)	191
Anna Simpson (11)	191
Aine O'Donnell (11)	192
Pascale Metcalf (11)	192
Nicole Noble (11)	193
Ruth Trick (9)	193
Daniel Blissett (10)	193
Laura Wood (11)	194
Ashley Skillington (11)	194
Grace-Ellen Burch (10)	195
Helene Payiatis (10)	195
Helen Ukoh (10)	196
Natasha Nasir (11)	197
Harriet Simpson (11)	198
Bethany Wilson (10)	198
James Tatt (10)	199
Emma Croft (11)	200
Sarah Griffin (10)	200
Georgina Skillington (9)	200
Tramaine Higgins	201
Jamil Jeffreys (9)	201
Jake Shipley (10)	201
Joseph Martinicca (9)	202

Sharp Lane Primary School

Amy Clarkson (7)	202
Rebecca Cawood (11)	203

Colleen Mooney (8)	203
Sam Parker (10)	204
Launa Senior (7)	204
Christopher Day (10)	205
Beau Procter (11)	206
Abbie Elliott (11)	206
Simon Atkinson (10)	207
Jade Brierley (11)	207
Jonathan Watt (11)	208
Danielle Sugden (11)	209
Kyle Holmes 10)	210
Sophie Cass (8)	210
Natalie Gelderd (10)	211
Bethany Tench (8)	211
Casey Brown	212

South Milford School

Alex Irvin (10)	212
Betsy Mallett (10)	213
Robyn Tanner (10)	213
Matthew McHale (11)	214
Jodie Barker (10)	214
Dominic Hinchley (10)	215
Faye Glasby (10)	215
Patrick Dean (10)	216
Miles Featherstone (10)	217
Owen Wake (11)	217
Lauren Howley (11)	218
Joshua Phillips (10)	218
Jamie Baratt Winter (11)	219
Hayden Fitchett (10)	219
Lloyd Harrison (11)	220
Peter Denton (11)	220
Helen Twigg (10)	221
Jonathan Booth (11)	221
Emily Wilson (10)	222
Victoria Borradaile (11)	222
Katie Brittain (10)	223

Ben Humphris (9)   270
Jessica Harris (7)   270
Tina Walsh (8)   271
Anna Morgan (8)   272
Naomi Booth-Wade (8)   273

West End Primary School
Dominic Lowe (11)   274
Ryan Clarkson   275
Rachel Borkala (10)   276
Rebecca Hutchinson (11)   276
Benita Guest (10)   277
Ashley Miller (11)   277
Caroline Poulter (11)   278
Laura Mallinson (10)   279
James McKenzie (10) & Michael Ambler (11)   279
Lizzy McCarthy (10)   280
Katie Farrar (10)   281
Daniel Barron (11) & Alistair McKenzie (10)   282
Cassandra Helen Quarmby (11)   282
Natalie Falls (11)   283
Rebeccah Yeadon (10)   284
Benjamin Vickers (11)   285
William Leung (10) & Matthew Wilkinson (11)   286
Conor Lowson & Jordan McKenna (10)   286
Corie Megan Jackson (10)   287
Lauren Cooke (11)   288
Alex Postle (11)   289
Alex Fitch & Jake Woodward (10)   290

The Poems

ALONE IN THE JUNGLE

My scaredness is taking over my body.
It is making my body shake like the Twin Towers did.
The trees are tall like a giant with a nasty grin on his evil face.
I can hear something walking.
The footprints look like a lion's footprints.
The sounds are beginning to gather.
They are bouncing off the trees.
My thirst is like a tramp's thirst with a dry tongue.
I see the lion. It has white, sharp teeth like juggling knives.
My nightmare is becoming a reality.

Natasha Stead (10)
Beeston Hill St Lukes CE Primary School

ALONE IN THE JUNGLE

I am lonely, I feel like my spirit has wiled away.
All I can see are suspicious trees that are angry and talking about me.
I can hear angry growls and trickling water with playful hands.
I have got nothing to eat, my thirst is a world with no water,
I can see reptiles and monkeys swinging from tree to tree,
Ants are crawling around me,
Waiting to bite like a crocodile waiting for meat.
My nightmares have become a reality.

Kimberley Appleton (10)
Beeston Hill St Lukes CE Primary School

ALONE IN THE JUNGLE

Sounds of the jungle echoing from the predators and prey.
My loneliness has set my spirit whirled away.
I see the animal grinding its teeth to attack.
My thirst has let my tongue become sandpaper.
The trees are staring and smirking at me.
My nightmares have become within my mind.

Manjeet Sagoo (10)
Beeston Hill St Lukes CE Primary School

ALONE IN THE JUNGLE

There are animals growling at me.
I can't see them, I can only hear them.
I see animals coming out of their hiding places.
My thirst and hunger is now showing.
My nightmare has unfortunately come true.
The trees are frowning and grinning at me.

Lucy Smith (9)
Beeston Hill St Lukes CE Primary School

ALONE IN THE JUNGLE

I'm scared, like all my fears put together.
Trees try to grab me with wickedness.
I'm not daring to go to sleep,
What with the greedy looks on the animals' faces.
Sounds of the jungle go creeping down my neck.
I'm starved like a dog that's never been fed.

Luke Longfield (9)
Beeston Hill St Lukes CE Primary School

ALONE IN THE JUNGLE

My loneliness is frightening me,
and my heart pounds like a cheetah running for freedom.

There are tigers staring at me, ready to attack me
now they are moving slowly and slowly.

My hunger is making my tummy rumble
like a lion growling in the distance.

The trees are around me, they are watching me
and whispering when they watch they watch every step I make.

The sounds of the jungle are terrible
whenever the sounds stop, my heart stops. Am I going to die?

Amrita Chana (10)
Beeston Hill St Lukes CE Primary School

ALONE IN THE JUNGLE

My senses buzz like a bee around a flower.
It's as though electricity flows through my veins.
The trees are as tall as horrible, staring giants.
My tummy is like a lion growling from a far distance.
The sounds of the birds and monkeys
Are like chitter-chattering chatterboxes.
I see iguanas with eyes like deep, dark pools of evil.
The ants march like sensible soldiers.
My spirit is alive, rustling through the tickling leaves,
The leaves are alive with me.

Cherlene Fung-Yao (10)
Beeston Hill St Lukes CE Primary School

ALONE IN THE JUNGLE

Trees are swaying and swirling,
They are the wind in the sky.
Thirst is the empty sea.
Sounds, sounds from the trees, sounds from where?
I can hear a jaguar growling at me.
I am scared and lonely,
No one to talk to, only the monkeys laughing at me.
I see jaguars, I see monkeys
While the ants nip and bite me.
My nightmares have come true.

Thomas Dawson (9)
Beeston Hill St Lukes CE Primary School

ALONE IN THE JUNGLE

My nightmares have become a reality.
I can see jaguars, tigers, ants.
The tigers growling, groaning fiercely.
Trees with green and red leaves,
The branches swaying like the arms of a grandad.
The sounds in the jungle are like an angry wind,
I am hungry, I need food
I can eat maggots, worms, even snakes.
I am scared and lonely by the morning.
I could be in a tiger's belly when it is starving.

Jessica Nicholson (9)
Beeston Hill St Lukes CE Primary School

ALONE IN THE JUNGLE

The trees are evil, and the branches are long and sharp as a knife.
My fear continues to grow like lava flowing fast from the mountain.
My nightmare is becoming alive.
My thirst is a dried up river bed,
And my mouth is like dead, dried bones.
The ants nipping my legs and they charge like soldiers all with food.

Victoria Howe-Young (9)
Beeston Hill St Lukes CE Primary School

ALONE IN THE JUNGLE

I woke up and I was in the jungle all alone.
The first thing I heard were the sounds of the jungle - terrifying.
The trees stared at me like I was a magnet to them.
I am so scared I feel like crying.
My hunger is the horse without any hay.
Nightmares are a reality for me.

Nathan Ripley (9)
Beeston Hill St Lukes CE Primary School

ALONE IN THE JUNGLE

Trees over my head like a hat glaring at me
Birds whistling and singing like a person
Terrible termites marching along like soldiers in battle
My thirst is the water now extinct from the world
My loneliness is a never-ending story.

Danielle Manderson (9)
Beeston Hill St Lukes CE Primary School

ALONE IN THE JUNGLE

Trees are grinning and glowing.
Wait, I hear something,
The bushes are ruffling and scruffling.
Fear touches me with cold fingers,
My mouth is as dry as sand,
Sticking my mouth together
And my stomach is rumbling
Like an earthquake.
My nightmares have come true,
Ants are crawling all over me
Like a marching army.

Iram Naz (10)
Beeston Hill St Lukes CE Primary School

ALONE IN THE JUNGLE

My loneliness is building up like a tower of bricks.
My fear is a dog shaking violently after a bath.
I see animals gliding from tree to tree,
Shredding, twittering and chatting noises
Pass through my ears.
The trees surround me as if I'm in a cage.
Sandpaper reminds me of my thirst
My nightmares become a reality when I wake up
In the middle of the night.

Jack Kilbride (9)
Beeston Hill St Lukes CE Primary School

JUNGLE

Alone in the jungle!
I'm all alone in the jungle,
I can only see trees and leaves.
The animals scream and screech
As if danger is coming towards them,
And their faces are confused
As though they have never seen my kind.
My fear continually grows
Like a hedgehog growing its spikes.
My thirst is the empty waterfall.
My hunger is like a lion growling
As if it's happy to see its prey.
The sounds of the jungle
Are like a whisper entering my ear.

Vittoria Vaccaro (9)
Beeston Hill St Lukes CE Primary School

ALONE IN THE JUNGLE

My loneliness is my companion and is a lost animal.
I can hear rustling in the bushes. Hello! Hello!
Hello anyone there?
The trees swirl and shake in the light breeze.
I see animals, ants crawling up my legs
Pinching me and birds whistling.
My thirst is the dry river bed,
My mouth is as dry as dead bones.
My worst nightmare is beginning to come true.

Robert Moore (9)
Beeston Hill St Lukes CE Primary School

ALONE IN THE JUNGLE

I'm so thirsty, my mouth is going to crack.
The trees are surrounding me and grinning at me.
I can hear birds twittering; it's a beautiful sound.
I see tigers, lizards and snakes,
Maggots on leaves are dropping on my head.
I am terrified; this is my worst nightmare.

Samantha Stockdale (10)
Beeston Hill St Lukes CE Primary School

ALONE IN THE JUNGLE

The trees are giving me horrible glares
I feel as lonely as a tree without leaves.
My hunger is a vegetable patch without vegetables.
The animals are talking in my ears
My nightmares are becoming true
The sound of the animals talking
Is like a person gasping for life.

Amethyst Kinnair (9)
Beeston Hill St Lukes CE Primary School

ALONE IN THE JUNGLE

My nightmare is beginning automatically.
My thirst is like an empty swimming pool.
Ants bite my blistering feet.
I'm surrounded by glaring trees
Which mock my misery.
I am alone with my fear.

Andrew Haigh (9)
Beeston Hill St Lukes CE Primary School

ALONE IN THE JUNGLE

I wake up to trees swaying in the lovely breeze,
the trees are grinning and laughing at me.

I am hungry in the jungle, my belly starts to growl.
I can't escape the hunger.

I am lonely in the jungle, I want a friend by me.
I want to find a way to escape my loneliness.

The sounds of the jungle are frightening right now.

Jaguars and lions are coming to catch me,
I run as fast and as far away as can be.

My nightmares become a reality, my nightmares come to life.
My nightmares come from my mind.

Stefanie Selby (10)
Beeston Hill St Lukes CE Primary School

ALONE IN THE JUNGLE

Trees! Trees! All around staring and glaring at me.
Jaguars growling, monkeys chattering and chattering,
Parrots squealing here or there.
My loneliness is cold and I feel in my heart
That I have been left out.
My tongue feels like it has been cemented on my lips
It feels as though not even a drop is left on land.
My stomach is mumbling and buzzing like bees.
I can't feel anything except my realisation
That my nightmare has come true.

Umer Shaikh (9)
Beeston Hill St Lukes CE Primary School

PARROTS

Parrots are colourful,
Parrots are bright,
They talk all day long
And sleep through the night.
They're smart and they're clever
And do lots of tricks,
They eat lots of fruit
And play with their sticks.

Stephanie Faulkner (11)
Bramley Christ the King Primary School

CINQUAINS

Something . . .
Falling from the
tree, falling, twirling and
dying, normally green I'm dead.
Help me.

Tony Plant (11)
Bramley Christ the King Primary School

SPRING CINQUAIN

Listen,
The raindrops are,
Falling, the flowers bloom,
The sun is going down. The night,
Is here.

Bethany Harrison (10)
Bramley Christ the King Primary School

EVACUEE

Frightening
in the quiet countryside.
Far away from my family
want to go home.
I miss my mum hugging me.
The waves are crashing against the rocks,
horses galloping beside me.
The wind blows smoothly,
missing the smell of the stairs
as I quietly go past the other houses.
Will I ever go home?
frightening.

Rebecca Harrison (10)
Bramley Christ the King Primary School

THE EVACUEE

Fear.
All around is unknown.
The people just know me as the evacuee.
The strange silence sends a chill up my spine.
Leaves falling from the limp trees.
The ghostly wind rushing,
As if trying to get away.
Running along the endless road.
Footsteps.
Is it my imagination?
I tell myself, yes, yes, yes . . . no!

Sally Jackson (10)
Bramley Christ the King Primary School

MY MEDAL

Gold, shining in the sun,
Reflecting off my face,
Remembering my friends,
Putting it on my army bag,
Proud memories,
Tears fall down my face,
Thinking of my dead comrades,
Living in my heart,
They will never be seen again.

Rajhneet Gill (10)
Bramley Christ the King Primary School

THE YOUNG BABY OF YORK

There was a young baby of York,
Who was always stealing pork.
For he said, 'It's for my dad,
Or else he will go mad.'
That thieving young baby of York.

Conor Bradley (10)
Bramley Christ the King Primary School

CINQUAINS

Crashing . . .
bright yellow sand
people walking their dogs
children are playing with beach balls,
great day . . .

Imogen Enefer-Mann (11)
Bramley Christ the King Primary School

LITTLE BULLET

A small bullet,
Black with a silver tip,
Tied to a golden chain,
Some, just some,
Memories are great.
Then, thinking of my lost partners,
Washes out my lonely mind.
Why? Where? Who?
They went like *snap!*
Forever lost.
Never to be found.

James Cusack (11)
Bramley Christ the King Primary School

A CAR POEM

Mid 40s' model
Needs few repairs
Got a couple of grey hairs - needs a respray
Very, very stressed engine.
Crashes into walls all the time.
Has very big wheels.
Likes tooting his horn.
Needs re-tuning
Passed its MOT
The colour of the car is brown.
I call it Mr Daly.

James Clayton (11)
Bramley Christ the King Primary School

MY EVACUEE ESCAPE

Sorrow
The sadness painting me into a dull, empty landscape
The evacuations have spoilt my life
And taken me into a path of ruin
Wild waves beating at rough rocks in the distance
The wind gripping me with cold hands
The trees around me sway sadly in the darkness
The home I always knew
Sticks in my head
Disappearing, leaving me . . .
Leaving my mind . . .
Leaving me alone
Chills run up and down my spine
As I walk on through moonlit paths
And the wind yawns again,
Following me.

Deanna Marie Hatton (11)
Bramley Christ the King Primary School

THE BULLET

The rusty rim,
The golden shine glittering off the moon,
The bullet that killed him,
My friend,
My best friend,
He helped me but I didn't help him.
Now it's locked up in my thick metal safe
But now he's gone,
Gone forever.

Adam Newby (10)
Bramley Christ the King Primary School

MY PROTECTOR

My protector, my protector,
Sharp and invisible to the eye,
One silver bullet loads, to fire at the precise time,
One, one single silver spark fired into the darkness,
One look is filling my head with blood,
Balancing in my attic
When I look into the eye,
My head spins with madness,
Memories of my mother,
Memories of my father,
All gone.

Jordan Walker (10)
Bramley Christ the King Primary School

MY KNIFE

My knife, my knife,
silver-bladed, brown-handled,
dark memories of the war returning,
how we won,
but how we lost,
memories of fellow comrades,
who lost their lives,
never,
never to return.

Luke Muffitt (10)
Bramley Christ the King Primary School

A BLITZED STREET

I could hear the shrieking of women and children,
The explosions of bombs and the crunching of a raging fire.
I could smell conflict, brutality, but worst of all, war.
I could taste no more electricity in the air,
But replacing it - bitterness, the fires were so strong
Now I could taste the ash.
I leaned out to touch a wall
But instead I felt rubble and fire,
I touched my face, and even next to fire it was ice-cold.
I opened my eyes and saw death . . . utter death.

Eugene Falconer (11)
Bramley Christ the King Primary School

MY SPECIAL ONE

She reminds me of the colour yellow for she is so bright.
She reminds me of a hot summer's day.
She reminds me of a blazing heat that makes me sweat.
She is a soft pillow on which I rest my head.
She is a big fluffy chair which I sit on.
She reminds me of a heartbeat because that's what my heart does.
She also reminds me of a sweet, delicious muffin.
My special one is Sian.

Samuel Richardson (11)
Bramley Christ the King Primary School

DIAMOND

To my lost companions I said,
'If we never meet again,
have this glistening diamond,
that gave me happiness
and joy through my life.

When you look into it,
it will show
I am always with you.
Shiny, fragile.

Never forget me
or my diamond.
Oh shiny diamond,
as we drift apart
I will, I will remember
my shiny, glistening diamond
and you as my comrades.'

Angelica Sykes (10)
Bramley Christ the King Primary School

A . . .

A person with two hands,
A baby that can only count to twelve.
A bomb that doesn't stop ticking.
A picture that hangs on the wall.
A sounding alarm.
A catalogue to make a . . . clock.

George Grant (10)
Bramley Christ the King Primary School

MY BULLET

My bullet, my bullet,
Hanging on a cold, silver chain.
Given to me by the sergeant.
Cold memories, happy memories.
Sadness, tears trickle down my cheek
As I think of all my fellow friends,
Who died in the terrifying battle against Germany.
Lonely,
In their shivering, soil-covered graves.

Daniel Waite (10)
Bramley Christ the King Primary School

MY BULLET

My bullet
Shiny, gold and silver.
Locked securely in my cupboard,
Nothing as neat
My prized possession,
Gleaming like a mirror.
Bringing back my sad, sad memories.
All my dead comrades not here, but not forgotten,
They gave their lives for worthless, worthless us,
Shelled and shot, I survived.

Carl Rushforth (11)
Bramley Christ the King Primary School

MY ADVERT POEM ABOUT MY BIG BROTHER

2000 big bro,
Bit rusty, needs a lot of
Work, annoying . . . desperately
Needs respray and facelift. Bit rough,
Thinks he's a Jaguar,
Really an old banger,
Swap for anything.

Sian McMullan (11)
Bramley Christ the King Primary School

SMITH CAN YOU SCORE?

Smith was playing football like he'd never played before,
When I tapped him on his shoulder to see if he could score
'Smith can you score, can you score, can you Smith?'
When he looked at me with one eye and took a big sniff
'I'm the best scoring Smith this world's ever seen,
I'm a shout, shout, goal, goal, score, score king!'

And he took a deep breath and ran across the pitch
And started to score with a *bim, bam boom!*
And he changed his position and span upon his hand
And as he slowed down this is what he said.
'I'm the best scoring Smith this world's ever seen,
I'm a shoot, shoot, scream, scream, score, score king!'

Then he got it round David Beckham and got it round Roy Keane,
Then he got it round Van Nistelrooy and scored, scored, scored,
He scored not using his legs, he scored not using his head,
But he's the best scoring Smith this world's ever seen.
'I'm a shoot, shoot, scream, scream, shout, shout, goal, goal,
Score, score king!'

Jack Gillespie (9)
Bramley St Peter's CE Primary School

THE FOOTBALL PLAYER

Kewell can you score?
Kewell was on the pitch, he was scoring.
When I tapped him on the shoulder to see if he could score
Kewell, can you score, can you score? Can you Kewell?
He said to me, 'Man I am the best scorer-player
In the world for a score-scorer,
Tap, tap, score, score, player.'

And he came off the pitch in the top corner of the pitch.
And he started to score with a hip-hop
He ran around and around
And smiled with cheer
And he ran around, what he said is,
'I'm the best scorer the world's ever seen
I'm a score-score hip-hop, score-score player.'

Matthew Johnson (9)
Bramley St Peter's CE Primary School

HEAD PAINS

Someone shouts in my ear.
I want to shout into hers.
It pumps, it thumps, it knocks too,
I want to go home, I really do,
I cry all day, the pain gets worse,
I feel like I'm going to burst,
Pressure pumps in my veins,
1, 2, 3, 4, 5, 6, 7, 8, 9, 10.
I feel I'm going to . . .
I'm alive again.

Lauren Hutchinson (10)
Bramley St Peter's CE Primary School

IT'S NOT THE SAME ANYMORE

It's not the same anymore since Floppy died,
carrots are carrots.
Never given since, never eaten.

It's not the same anymore,
sawdust lays still, never moves.
I've not got any energy to stroke.

It's not the same now,
I can't bring myself to laugh.
There's no reason to do so.

Her collar's on a hook
and her name tags are all dusty.

Her hutch and bowl are in the shed,
lying at an angle in the shed.

My old little teddy will never be chewed,
I have no excuse for not eating my carrots.

I can watch TV in peace, uninterrupted,
no frantic runs and leaping, just when it's exciting.

Danielle Pinkney (10)
Bramley St Peter's CE Primary School

LIGHTNING

Thunder, rain, they're all the same
Lightning's bad, it makes me sad.
You might think I'm quite silly
But I'm not, it's the truth.
Lightning, it's frightening.

Dane Hiscocks (9)
Bramley St Peter's CE Primary School

OVERHEAD IN THE HEAVENS

'Angel, Angel what are your pearls?'
'White glass, Fairy. Why do you stare at them?'
'Give them to me.'
'No.'
'Give them to me, give them to me.'
'No.'

'Then I will scream all night in the clouds.
Lie on my bed and howl for them.'
'Fairy, why do you love them so?'

'They are better than night and day.
Better than silver and gold.
Better than I can say.
Please let me have them to hold.'

'Hush, I stole them from my mother's wardrobe.'
'Give me your beads, I want them.'
'No!'
'I will scream in the underground
For your white glass pearls, I love them so.
Give them me, give them me.'
'No!

I need them to pay the king,
So I can keep my home,
I will swap my ring
And give you my gnome.'

Sapphire Walker (10)
Bramley St Peter's CE Primary School

OVERHEARD ON A CLOUD

'Angel, Angel, what is your harp?'
'Gold and rubies, Dove, why do you stare at it?'
'Give it to me.'
'No.'
'Give it to me, give it to me.'
'No.'
'Then I will cheep all night on the moon,
Lie on the soft clouds and howl for it.'
'Dove, why do you love it so?'

'It is better than the white snow,
Better than a cry of a bird,
Better than arrows and a bow,
Better than the feathers of a golden bird.'

'Hush, I stole it from my mother's chamber.'
'Give me your harp, I want it!'
'No.'
'I will cry on the clouds
For your harp with rubies, I love it so.
Give it to me, give it to me.'
'No!'

Devon Coates (10)
Bramley St Peter's CE Primary School

I LOVE ANIMALS

I love animals, they're sweet and cuddly,
I love spiders, they're tiny as can be.
I love cats, they're furry, that's for me,
I love dogs, they're lovely and eat more than Leeds.
I love animals, I close my eyes,
I am in a world of wonderland.

Loutia Kay (10)
Bramley St Peter's CE Primary School

TEARS

Tears dripping down my face,
Splashing on the ground,
Exploding like a magnificent firework.
What a beautiful sound.

I'll never forget her,
She's ever so sweet and kind.
The woman, her name . . . Gran
Is always on my mind.

Amy Walker (10)
Bramley St Peter's CE Primary School

FLOWER

Red as a rose.
Orange as a dandelion.
Purple as a tulip swaying in the breeze.
Yellow as a sunflower.
White as a rose I grow in a shower.
Blue as a bluebell, shining nice and bright.
I am the sun, I am very light.
Beautiful like lavender, *sniff*
I smell the sweet Cherish perfume.

Samantha Dennis-Bartle (9)
Bramley St Peter's CE Primary School

CARS

I am a car, smoke flying out of the back.
Out of the engine, going over the hill the oil falls out.
The car slipping all over the place.

Ryan Wilson (10)
Bramley St Peter's CE Primary School

THE COLOURFUL RAINBOW

Colourful rainbow filling the sky
With sparkling colours such as:
Red like a ruby,
Yellow like a buttercup,
Green like the lovely grass
And the orange sunset going down.
Purple tulips growing in the ground,
The pink blossom that caught my eye,
Last but not least, blue like a bluebell
And you can't ever forget
The sparkling rainbow that caught my eye.

Stephanie Marston (9)
Bramley St Peter's CE Primary School

WINTER

Winter
Winter is here.
It came today
And we're going outside to play.
Snowflakes drop on the trees
And a cool winter's breeze,
The snow's soft
The ice is hard
Let's all write a Christmas card.

Jake Webber (10)
Bramley St Peter's CE Primary School

I'M A BEE

I'm a bee flying in the air
Looking for a yummy flower
When I fly
I see the world
From above
Lots of people are scared of me
But I'm just a harmless bee
In actual fact
I'm terrified of you
Please don't hurt me
Or I'll have to sting you!

Abigail Cliff (10)
Bramley St Peter's CE Primary School

SPIDERS

Spiders are crawling all around.
I feel scared, they're all closing me in,
If they move I scream.
They're black and hairy,
Always scare me
But they're more scared of me.
They're in your bath,
They're everywhere!

Kailey Jane Edwards (9)
Bramley St Peter's CE Primary School

THE MAGIC BOX
(Based on 'Magic Box' by Kit Wright)

I will put in the box . . .
the action of small figures
and my awesome friends to keep me company
and my dark blue hat.

I will put in the box . . .
dazzling golden trophies
a melted piece of cheeze pizza and
some fragrant gel pens to smell.

I will put in the box . . .
a polished birth ring from when I was born
and memorable postcards from friends
and a small piece of fur from my dog, Max.

I will put in the box . . .
the magic of a golden beach
a sparkle of a twinkling star and
the face of an old friend.

Michael Hunter (10)
Bramley St Peter's CE Primary School

FOOTBALL CRAZY

Football flying through the air,
You shoot for a striking dare,
Oh yes said the mayor.
See glories, see pride,
There's David Beckham, hide!
I wish to be a footballer,
When I'm a lot taller.

Michael Ash (9)
Bramley St Peter's CE Primary School

MY CAT, SLY

My cat is dying,
He will be lying,
In the ground
Where there is no sound.
His name is Sly,
He makes me cry,
I don't know why,
But he's dy ing.

He will be leaving me,
As you can see,
I will cry every day,
You'll hear me from far away.

Laken Scholey (10)
Bramley St Peter's CE Primary School

MY ANNOYING SISTER

My room is a mess
I try to sleep but I'm in some stress
I listen to music on my own
As my sister's on the phone
Ha ha ha hee he he,
That's my sister laughing
So I can't sleep.
I toss and turn because my sister is too loud
And will never learn!

Sheridan Mackey (9)
Bramley St Peter's CE Primary School

IT'S NOT THE SAME SINCE MY FISH DIED

I don't see my fish anymore
He's not with me. There's no more swimming,
no more bubbles I can watch,
no more black fish I see.
No more fish food to buy with my pocket money.
No more black fish I see.

I can't laugh at the funny things he did
topples and turns he would learn.
Every morning he would jump over the water and back in.
He always knew when I was going to bed.
No more black fish I see.

Kirsten McGann (9)
Bramley St Peter's CE Primary School

RAINBOW

Magical rainbow high in the sky
With bursting colours that caught my eye.
Red is a rose
Yellow is a buttercup
Pink is a girl
Green is the grass
Orange is the sunset
Purple is a tulip
Blue is the sky
And that is the rainbow
That caught my eye.

Chelsea Wood (9)
Bramley St Peter's CE Primary School

FLOWERS

I am a small seed
buried in the ground
searching for some light

My shoot pops up
I can nearly see the light
pushing, pushing, pushing
I am nearly there
water, water, water me

I am at the top at last
look at my lovely colours
let me spread my aromatic smell

Red, pink, orange too
purple, red and light blue.

Jade Dixon (10)
Bramley St Peter's CE Primary School

HALLOWE'EN

Look around, what can I see?
People dressed up just like me
Knock at the door or ring the bell
See if you can make the people yell
You get candy, crisps and sweets
Believe me you will get heaps and heaps
People dress up like witches, devils, and cats
The witches usually wear their fake hair and their hats.

Natasha Scott (9)
Bramley St Peter's CE Primary School

THE GOONIES

They crossed the road in a dustbin lid,
In a dustbin lid they crossed the road,
In spite of what the people said,
One fell out and bumped his head,
In a dustbin lid they crossed the road,
When the lid rocked side to side,
One got out then went back inside,
One called out, 'Our lid's too small
But we don't care, we don't care at all.
In a dustbin lid we'll cross this road.'
Far and few, far and few are the lands where the Goonies go,
Their eyes pop out and their bodies are blue
And they crossed the road in a dustbin lid.

Ryan Scott (9)
Bramley St Peter's CE Primary School

ISABELL, ISABELL

Isabell met a hissing snake,
Isabell, Isabell didn't care for cake.
The snake's tongue was forked, the snake itself was mean
And his venom was gooey and green.
The snake said, 'Isabell, how do you do?
I'm sorry, but I have to eat you!'
Isabell, Isabell did not fret,
While the snake waved a fishing net.
She looked at the snake and waggled her head,
Then accidentally stood on the snake's head!

Faye Haseltine (10)
Bramley St Peter's CE Primary School

MY FAVOURITE 3 ANIMALS

Dolphins are cute,
flying through the air.
Helping tired swimmers,
all over and everywhere.

Horses have fun,
galloping in the sun.
Running all over,
meeting everyone.

Polar bears are white,
warm and woolly.
At the North Pole,
they're always funny.

Holly Walton (9)
Burton Salmon CP School

MY DOG

My dog is chocolate coloured
her eyes and nails are too.
At Christmas time we paint her nails
to make them sparkly too.
She drinks my cups of tea
and eats my dinner too.
She sleeps on my mum's bed
and chews my sister's teds.
She eats the mail, chases her tail,
whizzes around like something unreal.
But I love my Jazz
she's the bestest pet.

Joe Gardner (11)
Burton Salmon CP School

WHAT ARE BONFIRES AND FIREWORKS?

A bonfire is a glowing monster
from the unknown land,
fireworks are stars cramped together
fallen from the Milky Way.
A bonfire is a tent of light
out on a night trip,
fireworks are loud glitter shapes
dancing in the sky.
A bonfire is a flame's den
to hide away from light,
fireworks are cascades of sparks
lighting up the dark night sky.
A bonfire is Guy's home
to burn down to ash
and to watch the phoenix rise again.

Jessica Hunter (11)
Burton Salmon CP School

THE MOON

The moon is like a big sphere
moving across the silent sky
like some moonbeams.
It looks ever so lonely.

Its craters look grey
but the moon sparkles.
It looks mysterious.
It is so peaceful.

Lauren Watson (9)
Horsforth St Margaret's CE Primary School

THE MOON

The full moon

The moon glows
Like a gigantic marble.
The eye of the night
Gazes down on the Earth.
The monster moon shimmers
Like a diamond.

The crescent moon.

The moon is
Like a silver earring
Dropped from another universe,
Shiny as a fishing hook.

Brett Fisher (8)
Horsforth St Margaret's CE Primary School

THE MOON

Glittering, sparkling, glowing in the night
Like a night-time dwarf it shimmers with light.

The moon is spooky, shivering in the night,
Slowly disappearing, it shimmers with light.

The silver moon is glittering in the night,
Like a lump of cheese it shimmers with light.

The shiny moon sparkling in the night
Like a shiny wheel it shimmers with light.

Philip Hickman (9)
Horsforth St Margaret's CE Primary School

THE MOON

The moon is illuminating
in the pitch-black sky.
The moon is like
a big white balloon.
The moon gives off
a bright light.

The moon is as
silent as a mouse.
Some people are scared
of the moon but
others like the moon.
When the moon
goes to bed
the sun comes
out to play.

Daniel Greenway (9)
Horsforth St Margaret's CE Primary School

THE MOON

The full moon

As big as a football,
As shiny as a diamond ring,
As big as a cotton wool ball,
Like a clock with no hands and numbers,
Like a big chunk of cheese.

The crescent moon

The crescent moon is like a white banana,
Like a boomerang floating in the sky.

Jordan Richmond (9)
Horsforth St Margaret's CE Primary School

THE MOON

The moon is like a football,
As bright as beams,
Like something unique flowing in the sky,
As illuminating as fireworks,
The moon shimmers like silver,
As symmetrical as a circle,
As mysterious as a ghost.

The crescent moon is like a banana,
As silver as a ring,
Like a crystal,
Like a massive balloon,
It sneaks from the sky.

Charlotte Green (9)
Horsforth St Margaret's CE Primary School

THE MOON

The full moon

The moon glows
like a giant marble.
The eye of the night
never sleeps.
The monster moon is as
cold as a snowball.

The crescent moon

The moon is like a boomerang
hanging above the world.
The moon is as shiny
as a hook.

Billy Simpson (9)
Horsforth St Margaret's CE Primary School

THE SILVER MOON

Silver, shining is the moon,
Floating round, drifting up.
Silver, shining is the moon,
Like a great big, white balloon.

Silver, shining is the moon,
Perfectly spherical.
Silver, shining is the moon,
Reflecting like a silver spoon.

Silver, shining is the moon,
Illuminating bright.
Silver, shining is the moon,
Unique and aged, like a rune.

Silver, shining is the moon,
Mysteriously silent.
Silver, shining is the moon,
He'll come back to see us soon.

Lois Brown (8)
Horsforth St Margaret's CE Primary School

THE SILVER MOON

Wacky is the moon,
Cracky is the moon,
Spooky is the moon
And silver is the moon.
As cheesy as Wensleydale,
As silver as a rail.
I can see the man on the moon,
He is shining like a ruby.

Jonathan Bargh (9)
Horsforth St Margaret's CE Primary School

THE MOON

It sparkles in the night
Like a newborn diamond
My eyes start to shine
When I look out my window.

As round as a ball
And just as hard as a wall
The sun has gone to bed
Because the night is dead.

If I was the moon
I would show off my power
And I would wear a scarf
But not like the moon, because it is bare.

Now the sun is coming out
The moon goes to bed
As I fall asleep
In my warm and cuddly bed.

Lucinda Layfield (9)
Horsforth St Margaret's CE Primary School

THE MOON

'As shiny as a silver spoon,
Just like a big, white balloon,
It's made out of cheese,
As round as peas,
Quieter than me,
Higher than a tree,
But it fades away
At the start of the day,'
Said all the stars to the moon.

Alice Perfettini (8)
Horsforth St Margaret's CE Primary School

THE MOON

The full moon

The moon is a gigantic marble
With the colour of a ghost.
Glaring at you from up above
Like a flying eye up in the sky.
Moving minute by minute
Through the dark, foggy sky
With its eye never blinking.

The crescent moon

The moon is like a shiny silver earring
Hanging in the sky like a giant.
Boomerang spinning around
As shiny as a silver fishing hook.

Lewis Naiff (8)
Horsforth St Margaret's CE Primary School

THE FULL MOON

The moon glows
Like a marble
The night eye
Never sleeps
The mother of all moons
The crescent moon
The moon is
Like a silver smile
It's like a baby's mobile
Over the crib of the Earth
Plucking a tail feather
From the night sky.

Luke Jowsey (9)
Horsforth St Margaret's CE Primary School

THE FULL MOON

The moon rises big and white
to protect the stars,
like a silvery caring mum
at night-time.

The moon is shining
quietly circling the Earth,
like a yummy marshmallow
everyone is still fast asleep.

The moon playing
like a beachball,
bouncing in space.

William Caress (9)
Horsforth St Margaret's CE Primary School

THE MOON

The moon is like a glowing skeleton
hanging in the sky.
It's like a smiling face.

It's like a football
bouncing around the sky.
A warm hole in the night sky.

A round silver button in the sky.
There's no gravity on the moon
you cannot jump as high as the Earth.

Abigail Grant (9)
Horsforth St Margaret's CE Primary School

THE NIGHT'S EYE

An eye appears,
big and round watching,
watching the children.
Looking after the sweet
dreams of their sleep.

An eye peeks out,
glowing bright.
Like a white eye watching
the children as they toss
and turn in their sleep.

An eye looks out,
her face is now pale,
like a white ball
that has not been
used for some years.

An eye now closing,
closing tight.
Is it the end of mother of night?

Lucy Stephens (8)
Horsforth St Margaret's CE Primary School

THE MOON

The moon is out all night
if you go out it will give you a fright.
The moon glows as you go down to the garden.
As cold as ice but the stars are as small as rice
as the moon is glistening again.
As the sun comes up the moon turns into dust
you finally wake up and you are happy all day.

Hannah Barker (8)
Horsforth St Margaret's CE Primary School

THE MOON

The misty moon rises.
The sun slowly drifts away,
like a feather.
Falling.

The moon sparkles.
Through the dark, gloomy clouds,
peeks the gigantic, glowing moon.
Lighting up the street.

The shadowy moon
is getting tired,
waiting for the sun.
Soon the sun will take over
the weary moon's job.

The sunset is rising
the moon is asleep
waiting to come out,
tomorrow.

Alice Pickering (8)
Horsforth St Margaret's CE Primary School

FULL MOON

Tonight the full moon is a face
that is staring at me
I think he is very bored,
because he is lonely.
The stars chase him all night,
that's why he's tired.
He's always moving around the world.
In the morning he's not there.

Joe Carroll (8)
Horsforth St Margaret's CE Primary School

THE FULL MOON

The moon rises,
as day turns into night.
It gazes at the stars
through the darkness.

The moon peeks through the dark clouds
pushed by the wind.

The moon dances
like a white disco ball in the sky.

The moon slips into the night.

The moon plays in the night.

The moon gleams in the deep, dark sky.

It shines like an oven plate.

Amy Dobson (8)
Horsforth St Margaret's CE Primary School

THE FULL MOON

The moon is like a sparkly disco ball
It is a globe, maybe a gobstopper.
It might be a grey button,
But we don't know what it looks like.

We can only see that it is powdery and round.
I think it looks like a head or a big, big apple.

Now I know that it is just
A rusty old moon.

Emily Woodgate (8)
Horsforth St Margaret's CE Primary School

THE NIGHT'S EYE

The gentle moon's light shines,
surprises the weary day.
Like a sudden joke, night.

Gazing at the Earth's spin,
the moon protects children's dreams,
guarding the night.
It's like a still disco ball hanging
from the sky.

The moon peeks through misty clouds,
like a sky thief.
Alone in the sky,
gleaming a soft, silvery light.

The moon sleeps,
creeps into misty clouds.
Smiling like a honey cat,
shadows dance under the moonlight.

The moon slips,
dips into day.
Like a closing mouth,
swallowing darkness.

Naomi Milton (8)
Horsforth St Margaret's CE Primary School

THE ANCIENT MOON

The ancient moon is as still as the dead
and older than them too,
time's scars mark its face.

It is like a giant balloon or a glowing lamp
with a shadow-filled past
like a giant black hole.

It watches over everyone
as they have their shut-eye.
Dark is the criminal
the moon has its stolen light,
bright as gold.

Like an eye saying night, night!
Guard of the shadow prisoners.

Jack Baker (9)
Horsforth St Margaret's CE Primary School

THE MOON

The moon shines at night.
It is like a big, white ball.
The moon rises at night.

A football kicked
into the sky at night,
shining like a disco ball.

A flame burning,
there is no gravity.

Matthew Evans (8)
Horsforth St Margaret's CE Primary School

THE MOON

The full moon

The moon glows
like a giant marble,
the eye of the night
never sleeps,
the monster mother
of all moons

The crescent moon

The moon is
like a silver earring
dropped from another universe,
it stays in the sky
with a silent smile,
as shiny as a pirate's hook,
the ghost of the moon.

Rebecca Cantlow (9)
Horsforth St Margaret's CE Primary School

THE FULL MOON

The full moon is like a disco ball,
twinkling in the night sky.
The moon gazes down
on the weary children in their beds,
watching over their nightmares.
The gleaming moon
shines on the sleeping people.
The moon slips into cool shade,
like a cat.
The moon fades away.

Chelsea Birdsall (9)
Horsforth St Margaret's CE Primary School

THE MOON RISES

The moon rises,
surprises the weary evening light.
Like a humorous joke.
Midnight.

The moon sneaks,
peeks through curtains drawn tightly.
Like mother of the night,
protecting her children's dreams.

The moon drifts
gently through the dark blue sky.
Like a lonely hanging disco ball.
Children sleep.

The moon shines
spinning through the misty clouds.
Like a lighthouse shining forever.
Dawn.

The moon dips,
sinks into the sea of light.
Like a petal falling off of a flower.
Morning.

Isobel Ridsdale (8)
Horsforth St Margaret's CE Primary School

THE MOON

The sun has gone to bed
The moon is like a silver orb
And all the day is dead.

The moon is drifting across the sky
As white as a ghost
As it floats by.

Illuminous light
Turns everything silver
What a beautiful sight.

Lighting up the clouds
As they go by.

Jessica Russell (8)
Horsforth St Margaret's CE Primary School

THE MOON

As the moon rises it shimmers
Then it starts waxing.
By this time it's a big, white balloon,
As silver as a wheel,
It starts glowing, it begins to stand out,
Then it starts waning,
The colours and the brightness begin to fade,
To the end of the day,
Then it sets as the sun rises.

Helen Wilson (8)
Horsforth St Margaret's CE Primary School

THE SOMETHING

The something looks edible,
as a big lump of cheese,
as big as a white button,
it must make you sneeze.

The something looks unique
it's glaring straight at you,
like a big, white reflection,
or a big, silver spoon.

Different shapes,
different sizes,
different colours,
it's as silent as can be.

The sun comes up,
the something goes behind,
let's all get up now
and start the day again.
What am I?

Emma Jeffries (9)
Horsforth St Margaret's CE Primary School

THE MOON

As glowing as a star
as white as a moon
as mobile as a car
as round as a balloon
as hard as a rock
as bumpy as a crater
as silver as a lock
as quiet as the wheel of a roller skater.

Rosie Baker (9)
Horsforth St Margaret's CE Primary School

THE MOON

The moon is like a silver button
And it's always glowing
The moon is always shimmering
And it's worth knowing.

The moon is like a big balloon
I think it's very bright
It's always still and silent
It must be a giant nightlight.

Sometimes it's very cheesy
It could be dripping wet
I think it's captivating
But it's nothing like a net.

Jessica Womack (8)
Horsforth St Margaret's CE Primary School

THE MOON

The moon is a mysterious thing
it sparkles like a diamond ring,
the moon is like a big, white ball
up in the sky it looks really tall.

Lighting up the seven seas
like a big hunk of cheese
like a big cotton ball
like a round, round wall.

The night is a little fright
in its illuminating light.

Oliver Calimer (9)
Horsforth St Margaret's CE Primary School

THE MOON

As the snowflakes fall on the town,
The moon overlooks the mountain.
He gazes down at the bright lights,
With large, round, droopy eyes.
Longing to be a child again,
A tear of moonlight -
Trickled down his soft, yellow cheeks,
And splashed down onto the mountain peak.
Children and parents join hands around -
The Christmas tree and merrily sing joyful carols.
The moon longs to join in,
But knows his days on Earth are long gone.
And, instead of grieving,
Happily watches them with a warm, glowing smile.

James Bell (11)
Horsforth St Margaret's CE Primary School

THE MOON

Sparkling, silver moon,
peeping through the clouds,
like a giant big balloon,
never to come down,
sparkling, silver moon shining,
3D light
like a huge ball of foil,
brightening up the night.

Sara Pickering (8)
Horsforth St Margaret's CE Primary School

ROLLING RACING

Rolling, racing down the road
My mum says I'll catch a cold.

I don't care, I'll survive,
I'll carry on racing while I'm alive.

So I've decided to set a trap,
So my mum does not get mad.

Turn the clocks back an hour
And when I get back I'll have a shower.

I'll rinse off all the mud,
Then I'll look better than good.

So I decided to try my plan the next day,
But things didn't go my way.

Kirsty Toomes (10)
Horsforth St Margaret's CE Primary School

THE MOON

As shiny as a silver spoon
As solid as a rock
As round as a balloon
As bright as a light
As mysterious as a haunted house
As sparkly as a diamond ring
As bumpy as a crater
As quiet as a mouse.

Emily Hall (9)
Horsforth St Margaret's CE Primary School

THE SILVERY MOON

The moon is like a white face,
watching over everyone,
as they close their eyes.
Protecting children as it turns to night.

The moon is like a glowing,
circular, silver disco ball,
shining in the sky.
Surrounded by golden stars,
the moon is like a glistening diamond.

The moon is like a great big star!
Shining here, there and everywhere.
I like the moon because it's bright
and comforts me through the night.

Naomi Metcalfe (9)
Horsforth St Margaret's CE Primary School

STATIONERY

Oh ruler, oh ruler, king of all measurements,
How your shatterproof form glistens in the light,
Unfortunately from your work,
You get battered, scratched and worn.

Eraser, eraser, unknown is your shape,
But you are affected by every mistake,
You're a dazzling sight when your colour's bright white,
But when you are dirty, you're not quite so perky.

Jacob Womack (10)
Horsforth St Margaret's CE Primary School

THE FULL MOON

The moon shines,
Another day has gone,
Like a snowball,
Night-time.

The moon's glow,
Gives dim light,
Like a white plate.
Moon's up.

The moon looks out,
Peeks through a thick cloud,
Like a flying football.
With the stars.

Mark Rawlinson (9)
Horsforth St Margaret's CE Primary School

THE FULL MOON

The full moon shines like a round beach ball
in the dark purple sky.
The moon is white like a white, glittering star,
a snowball that never melts because it's cold and frosty.
It hangs out of the sky like a paper lantern.
It gazes down at all the people,
protecting the children all night long
and their goodnight dreams.
Now it's time the moon goes down
and the sun comes up.

Matangi Patel (9)
Horsforth St Margaret's CE Primary School

THE FULL MOON

The moon rises,
surprises the day
like a funny joke.
Darkness.

> The moon creeps,
> sneaks through the misty clouds.

> > The silvery-white face
> > looks down to the town
> > to keep the children's dreams safe.
> > The moon spins like a disco ball in a party.

Sanderson Lam (9)
Horsforth St Margaret's CE Primary School

THE MOON

The moon is like a glowing skeleton,
hanging in the sky,
it is like a smiling face.

The moon is like a football
bouncing around the sky,
it looks like a wormhole.

It is shaped like
a round, silver, fat button.

Joshua Falcon (8)
Horsforth St Margaret's CE Primary School

THE GLEAMING MOON

The gleaming moon
hanging in the midnight sky,
like a sparkling disco ball.
Guarding the glittering stars.

The colour of snow,
like a silver diamond.
Watching children in their dreams,
while they sleep peacefully.

The shape of a snowball
like a flying eye.
Waiting for morning to come,
the moon dips,
slips into morning.

Maria Cullingworth (9)
Horsforth St Margaret's CE Primary School

THE SILVERY MOON

As the moon rises
it glitters and shines upon the world.

The big silver moon snowball,
the stars are like lots of little diamonds
surrounding the moon.

This big disco ball,
hanging from the moonlit sky.

Amy Sheard (9)
Horsforth St Margaret's CE Primary School

THE MOON'S EYE

The moon flickers,
guarding the dark night,
like a floating football,
midnight.

The moon wobbles,
blasting hot light,
like a silver ball,
night's noon.

The moon relaxes,
shining through the dark sky,
like a battering ball,
alone in space.

The moon shines,
slips into a light cloud,
like a snowy bear,
lights weaken.

The moon fades,
goes out of the night,
like a white beach ball,
devouring the night.

Matthew Shaw (8)
Horsforth St Margaret's CE Primary School

THE MOON

Round and round
in darkness
like a big balloon.
Up with the stars
floats the silver moon.

Chazz McHale (8)
Horsforth St Margaret's 7CE Primary School

THE SUN

Children are playing under the sun,
having so much fun,
an orange ball kicked high in the sky,
looks like the sun flying up high.

In the park, all the dogs bark
as people joyfully run.
There are no clouds to come and go,
as people shout and scream *ho! ho!*

But now the sun is going down,
people are walking through the town,
to get back home, to wait and wait
for another fun day,
filled with sun and fun.

Hannah Dobson (11)
Horsforth St Margaret's CE Primary School

THE FULL MOON

The bright shining moon, like the London Eye,
flickers in the night.
It's face is shrouded by the misty cloud
as the guardian guards the night.

The gleaming moon, like a big beach ball,
twinkled in the night and then slowly,
it sank deep,
deep into the night.

Samuel Fairburn (8)
Horsforth St Margaret's CE Primary School

THE FULL MOON

The full moon is like a white ball
gleaming and glowing,
watching and guarding the night sky.
A silver moon is like a big balloon
standing and listening
for the children to come home.
Its reflections from the sun,
peeping through the clouds
when the sun is asleep.
A moon is like a disco ball
hanging still and silent.
Beaming its light all around the world
bringing hope and love.

Anna Sandham (8)
Horsforth St Margaret's CE Primary School

THE MISTY MOON

The misty moon rises,
as the sun goes down for the night.
The moon protects the children's dreams,
keeping them safe for the evening.

The moon guides the stars.
Floating around the Earth,
guarding all the people.

The misty moon slips down
as the sun appears for another day.
The sun sparkles on the Earth.

Amy Foster (8)
Horsforth St Margaret's CE Primary School

A BEAUTIFUL DREAM

Late at night Mum says, 'Sleep tight.'
I go far away and my mum's not in sight.
I'm eating sweets, I'm eating pie,
I'm drinking drinks from a buttercup.

Later on I see my friends,
Visions of them in a Mercedes-Benz.
I go for a ride
High up in the sky,
Sorcery, soaring,
Gliding high.

Time for school now,
I've come to the ground,
I've come to the ground,
Without making a sound.

Georgina Laws (10)
Horsforth St Margaret's CE Primary School

AS THE MOON RISES

A round, white crystal
glows in the purple sky.
Stars sparkle surrounding
the gleaming and glistening moon.
The sun producing light
is behind a silver diamond
which is reflecting light.
The misty moon creeps along the sky
getting ready to switch places with the sun.
Now the golden sun rises and everyone awakes.

Sarah Northfield (9)
Horsforth St Margaret's CE Primary School

JUPITER

I'm beautifully coloured
But I'm red-hot inside
With my powerful whirlwind spot
I'm the most powerful planet, in the massive sky.
I've seen many things through my reign
But the thing I've seen most is a lot of pain
So why can't you stop all your fighting
And get on with your lives?
For lives are not forever
So you have to make the most of them

With my powerful whirlwind I help you to survive
For I'm the toughest of all planets in the sky.
I'm flaming hot
And when it is windy, sand is all over.
You would never be able to survive,
I'm flaming red with black and brown
Clouds on my surface.

Matthew Barker (11)
Horsforth St Margaret's CE Primary School

ALONE

My mum shouts goodnight from the floor down below.
Then I drift off to a place where no one should go.
I have nightmares about sadness and sorrow.
Alone now I am till the dawn of tomorrow.
I hate going to sleep, exhausted I am.
I dream all day of what my dream will say.

Iona Griffiths (10)
Horsforth St Margaret's CE Primary School

WHAT IS THE SUN?

The sun is bright,
the sun is big,
all the reds are a beautiful thing.

The sun is hot,
the sun gives light,
when it shines it feels like a burst of dynamite.

The sun is the one,
the sun has the power
that grows all the beautiful flowers.

The ball of gas with the name of sun,
comes right down with the power of a gun.

The Earth spins around the sun like a clock,
the heat of the sun makes my head go *tick-tock.*

Matthew Temple (10)
Horsforth St Margaret's CE Primary School

WOBBLY JELLY

Wobbly jelly is fun to eat.
Wobbly jelly is a real special treat.
Wobbly jelly in your belly goes a long way.
Then I sit and wait for my mum to say,
'Guess what Josh? It's jelly today.'
As I eat my delicious jelly,
My belly goes all wobbly and plump.
The only problem from eating lots of jelly is . . .
It gives you a big bump at the front!

Josh O'Hara (10)
Horsforth St Margaret's CE Primary School

THE MONSTER UNDER MY BED

I'm dwelling with happiness
because today the monster under the bed
gets back from his holiday under the stairs,
I'm so happy that he's coming back
because he protects me
from the nasty monsters under my bed.
I bet they could bite off my head,
could those nasty monsters under my bed!
I hope he comes back soon
because if he doesn't I'll miss him very much,
like I miss Milly the ghost.
She went away when Mummy told me she wasn't real.
Mummy said the monster under the bed wasn't real either
and now he's gone too.

Natalie Fox (11)
Horsforth St Margaret's CE Primary School

THE SCHOOL RAT RACE

Brring, brring, brring, brring.
Goes the school bell and so the school rat race begins.
The children from Class 6 are all running out of the room.
Bumping and jumping, scuttling and shuttling,
Bumping and thumping into each other.
It's only 3.20pm, why are they all running?
They don't want to see their mothers.
'It's home time! It's home time!' they all shout.
There's not going to be a big school bout.
They are all running out and one falls over into some hay.
It's not as if they all hate school, or do they?

Tom Jeffries (11)
Horsforth St Margaret's CE Primary School

EVERY OTHER SUNDAY

Every other Sunday
I stand and wait
For my dad to get ready,
Down by the front door in the hall.

If the weather's fine
We play rugby or football.
When it rains we watch sports TV
Wondering who will win.

He asks me about school
And what I've done this week
But everything's different now
We seem to talk

Every other Sunday
Dead on half-past four
Me and my dad come back from rugby
Telling our winnings to everyone.

Alex Crowther (11)
Horsforth St Margaret's CE Primary School

HELL

Hell is like burning fury and anger inside you.
Hell is the colour of red, fresh blood.
Hell sounds like a boy's scream
As he falls off a cliff edge onto sharp rocks.
Hell feels like hands touching oven flames.
Hell smells like burnt toast and choking smoke.
Hell looks like red-hot rocks
Surrounded with lava lakes spitting.

Alexander Hall (11)
Horsforth St Margaret's CE Primary School

SQUIRREL SURPRISE

Life at home was never dull
For Jennifer, Joe and Jim.
They lived together in a tree
With a woodlouse called Deadly Slim.

The three Js, they were squirrels
With tails of deep red-brown
They loved to show them off
To the people of the town.

One day some boys came to their tree
To try and steal their conkers
Said Joe to Jim, 'Just look at them!
They're absolutely bonkers!'

The boys were trying to reach a twig
Nine feet up in the air
They climbed upon a weakened branch
But they weren't taking care.

The branch gave a mighty crack
The squirrels let out a squeal
One tubby lad came tumbling down
And erupted his most recent meal.

Another chap landed on his head
Knocked himself out cold
Said Jennifer to Joe and Jim
'They shouldn't be so bold!'

The moral of this story is
Keep your feet upon the ground.
Next time the victim could be you
There's a chance you won't be found!

Elise Johnson (11)
Horsforth St Margaret's CE Primary School

HOLIDAY IN THE SUN

The sea front
The sand is golden,
As golden as can be,
The children are playing and paddling in the sea,
The adults are bathing in the sun,
On the beach we always have fun,
The children are begging for ice cream,
The dads are making a football team,
So as you can see the beach is a special place to be.

The café
Our hotel is next to the sea,
There's a café on the front where we always have tea,
The food is nice,
At a very low price,
We always have tea near the sea.

The plane
The plane goes very high,
From the windows we can see the sky,
The sun is beaming down,
From the windows we can see our town,
Although it's still night,
It's a beautiful sight,
We have really enjoyed our holiday.

Simon Barker (11)
Horsforth St Margaret's CE Primary School

WHO?

Who's that rustling through the trees?
Knocking at the door?
Who rushed past me on the wooden floor?

As hard as I try to ignore
Crack!
A brick lay on the floor
A dark figure rushed past.
'Who's there?' I asked.

I heard some rustling just outside the kitchen door
I opened it
There were things on the floor
But nothing more.

As I went to bed I reviewed
What had happened while I was in the mood
The rustling
The knocking at my door
The brick that still lay on the floor.
The figure that rushed past
And all the while
In the dead of night
I was thinking, w*ho? Who?*

Andrew Pickering (11)
Horsforth St Margaret's CE Primary School

THE LONELY POEM

Old women, old women,
You are so old.
You stand all alone in the freezing cold.

Small child, small child,
How young you must be,
Sleeping alone under the old oak tree.

Poor man, poor man,
You live upon the streets,
Wish some day will pass a treat.

My friend, my friend,
You sit over there,
Waiting for someone to show some care.

Ellie Singleton (11)
Horsforth St Margaret's CE Primary School

THE NIGHT HUNTER

The wind was a giant, breathing upon the water still
The moon was the giant's eye, watching over the world
The road was a silver snake, curling around the hill
And the powerful stoat came trotting,
Up to the worn out hole.

Inside the hole the hungry stoat vanished,
Through the tunnels he went
And soon came out with a rabbit
Its body rigid and bent
And quickly the stoat started running, running
The stoat started running back to his old, old den.

Yannek Bendler (10)
Kirkstall Valley Primary School

RUGBY OR BALLET

Coach says, 'Pass to Bob,'
Mum says, 'Hold on tight,'
Coach says, 'Pass to Reece,'
Mum says, 'Pass to Kevin,'
Who to listen to. What to do.

Coach says, 'Stay up front,'
Mum says, 'Drop back,'
Coach says, 'Let Liam go acting half,'
Mum says, 'Go acting half,'
Who to listen to. What to do.

Coach says, 'Go low,'
Mum says, 'Go high,'
Coach says, 'Let Liam go marker,'
Mum says, 'Go marker Son,'
Who to listen to. What to do.

I just can't make my mind up,
Who to listen to.
I think I'll give up rugby
And take up ballet dancing!

Nathan Hargreaves (10)
Kirkstall Valley Primary School

Mum's Orders

My mum said, 'Clean,'
So I had to Hoover.
My mum said, 'Baby,'
So I had to move her.
My mum said, 'Beans,'
So I had to shop.
My mum said, 'Press-ups,'
So I had to drop.

My mum said, 'Bed,'
So I had to make it.
My mum said, 'Garbage,'
So I had to take it.
My mum said, 'Remotes,'
So I had to give 'em up.
My mum said, 'Food,'
So I had to cook.

My mum said, 'Clothes,'
So I had to iron.
My mum said, 'Presents,'
So I had to buy 'em.
My mum said, 'Nappy,'
So I said, 'No!'
My mum said, 'Come here,'
So I said, 'Uh oh!'

Letitia Archibald (11)
Kirkstall Valley Primary School

MY FRIEND AND I

My friend and I were training,
Training for our big race.
But she fell over and grazed her knee,
So Alex took her place.

My friend and I were exhausted,
Exhausted from staying up late.
So we didn't go to school that day,
But played with our friend Kate.

My friend and I were looking,
Looking at a shooting star.
Through an expensive telescope,
Which helped me see so far.

Daniel Robinson (10)
Kirkstall Valley Primary School

ELEGY ON THE DEATH OF AN ONION

Oh on the vegetable plot I found him,
Innocently lying, his friends around.
I stared longingly at his plump, brown skin,
Then rolled up my sleeves and bent down.

So I tugged him away from his family
And walked to my back garden door.
As I put him on my work surface,
He seemed to look scrumptious no more.

Then I took my knife and couldn't believe my ears,
He said, 'I've got a family too,'
But I just didn't listen because,
I really wanted my stew.

Hannah Leonard (10)
Kirkstall Valley Primary School

POPPY

He's strange and weird,
He's old and has a beard,
He's sad and stroppy,
His face is red, we call him Poppy,
He's brown and hairy,
He's cute, just like a fairy,
He's cool, and drinks from a cup,
And guess what, I just made him up!

Charlotte Carrick (10)
Kirkstall Valley Primary School

MY PET HAMSTER

My pet hamster
Lives in my house,
He once got mixed
Up with a little mouse.

My pet hamster
Is so cute, he hid
Inside my brother's boot.

My pet hamster
Loves his wheel,
When he's hungry
He eats his meal.

My pet hamster
Likes to sleep,
He curls up tight
When I try to peep.

Charlotte Wainwright (8)
Lawns Park Primary School

ELLECIA AND ANIMALS

E   is for elephant big and strong
L   is for lion whose strides are long
L   is lizard who camouflages in the trees
E   is for eagle who glides through the skies
C   is for chimps who eat all the fruit
I   is for insects who eat some plants
A   is for animals who are quiet.

Ellecia McLoughlin (8)
Lawns Park Primary School

WHY?

I look outside as the world goes by
and wonder why some people cry.
I look outside as the world goes by
and wonder why we have to die.
I look outside as the world goes by
I'm glad to know I'm safe inside.

Amy Florance Whitaker (8)
Lawns Park Primary School

SOPHIE AND THE SEA

S   is for the seashells sweeping on the sand
O   is for the octopus slithering in the sea
P   is for the penguins that we love to see
H   is for the holidays all sunny and bright
I   is for ice creams creamy and white
E   is for England surrounded by the sea.

Sophie Dickson (8)
Lawns Park Primary School

COLOURS

Where is red?
Red, red, red
As a rose.

Where is yellow?
Yellow, yellow, yellow
As the sun.

Where is pink?
Pink, pink, pink
As a sunrise.

Where is green?
Green, green, green,
As the grass.

Where is purple?
Purple, purple, purple,
As my crayon.

Where is orange?
Orange, orange, orange
As an orange.

Where is blue
Blue, blue, blue,
As the sea.

All these colours
Make the rainbow of the world.

Amy Robinson (9)
Lawns Park Primary School

SPECTACULAR SNOWMAN

Sparkling, shining, crystals everywhere,
Gleaming, smiling, fun here and there,
Snowman, snowman I adore
Everything you are.
Playing with you all day long,
Having fun all day long,
It's cold outside,
Let's stay inside,
Snowball fights with you and me
We're having fun all winter through!

Zoe Popple (9)
Lawns Park Primary School

FIREWORKS

Fireworks, fireworks,
You come out in the night.

Fireworks, fireworks,
You really give me a fright.

Fireworks, fireworks,
You shoot out of sight.

Fireworks, fireworks,
You are really bright.

Kim Taylor (8)
Lawns Park Primary School

My Dog Ronnie

I have a dog called Ronnie
and people think he is so bonny.
He is a chocolate-brown all the way down,
from his head to his toe
and in the dark, his eyes they glow.

We often go for walks
and sometimes we have private talks.
He looks at me and wags his tail
as we carry on our merry trail.

Ronnie is a naughty boy
he always tries to grab my toys
and boy does he make some noise.
But I do love him because he is my friend,
now my poem must come to an end.

Lucy Coultas (8)
Lawns Park Primary School

Mammals

M is for magnificent like a dolphin so bright
A is for animals that dance all night
M is for mice that eat the cheese
M is for monkeys that love climbing trees
A is for antelopes that jump so high
L is for lambs who love to spring along
S is for squirrel that loves eating nuts.

This is my poem that I hope you will love.

Jack Shell (8)
Lawns Park Primary School

BENJAMIN HOPE

There was a boy named Benjamin Hope
Who went to Boots for a bar of soap
His teacher Mr Brian Beck
Had looked at Benjie's dirty neck
And saw among the grease and grime
Potatoes growing in a line
Around his neck, behind his ears
Causing laughs and cruel jeers
Wherever Benjie seemed to be
The vegetables were clear to see!
Till soap and water solved his troubles
With a foamy sponge and clouds of bubbles.

Liberty Wightman (9)
Lawns Park Primary School

JESS

My dog Jess is a boxer dog.
She likes to run around and go for a jog.

She loves to lick you with her tongue
And loves to play out and have lots of fun.

I love her so much she is my best friend,
But I must admit, she sometimes sends me round the bend.

Jamie McKue (9)
Lawns Park Primary School

BEVERLEY'S BEDROOM

Ten smelly socks hidden under the bed.
Nine cuddly teddies standing on their heads.
Eight books on the shelf waiting to be read.
Seven pens, 'Don't get them on the bed,' Mum said.
Six pencils full of lead.
Five sparkling rings all in a row.
Four Teletubbies, one called Po.
Three trophies for singing.
Two dollies dancing
One you don't want to know . . .

Georgia Dean *(8)*
Lawns Park Primary School

MY FAMILY POEM

My mum likes wine,
She drinks it sometimes,
My dad likes bitter,
He says, it's better,
Claire likes pop,
She drinks it a lot
And then there's me,
I like a cup of tea!

Matthew Sorby *(8)*
Lawns Park Primary School

MY LOVE

My love for him has once gone again,
the ship has sailed away,
I would have done anything,
just to be with him once more.

I will always remember the first day
I laid my eyes on him,
and then it was time to say goodbye,
farewell my love, farewell.

Toni Bulger (10)
Lawns Park Primary School

MY GRAN

My gran has big curly hair
It's fluffy and golden brown
It sits on her head all day
Like a big, fat, golden crown
My gran has big square glasses
That sit on her nose
And they slip off her face
When she starts to doze.

Thomas Southwell (7)
Lawns Park Primary School

MY HAMSTER

I have a little hamster
Who has a little house
Sometimes he's mistaken
For a little mouse.
He is really cuddly and sweet
And his hobby is he likes to eat.
He always sleeps in his wheel
Then comes out for a meal.

Katie Keeligan (9)
Lawns Park Primary School

WORLD WAR III

First the bombs on their way,
Or tomato ketchup I might say,
Some of my toast soldiers go down,
Then my oranges go bouldering down.
I hit my target, it sets on fire,
Or should I say mustard that's dire.
He sends grenades over the wall,
Or Mum's eggs, this is a great brawl.
My enemy's weakened, what should I do?
The thought comes to me straight away,
I will pelt him with food.

The end is very near,
I chuck a potato in his ear.
He falls to the ground
With an almighty sound.
I am the winner like some,
Oh no, you clean up, here's Mum!

Alex Mavor (10)
Leeds Grammar School

A MAGICAL WORLD

In the land where no one knows,
Live pixies, fairies and talking toads,
Where centaurs dance and spirits prance,
There are many things of wonder.

Where dragons fly in golden skies
And dark things sound their hollow cries,
Serpents crawl and goblins squall
And evil sorcerers make plans.

In the land of magic and mystery,
Wizards scheme and witches plot,
Warlocks cruel, try to rule
As ghosts and ghouls haunt the night.

Kings and queens in castles strong,
Emperors in palaces grand,
Knights and princes do great deeds,
To make princesses pay heed.

A traveller sees golden halls and cities great
And dwarfs and elves and gnomes
Things of beauty, things of magic,
And wakes up! It was all a dream!

Or was it?

Sam Barnett (11)
Leeds Grammar School

THE SNAKE

The snake comes out in the dark
So in the dark don't go to the park
And when it eats someone it leaves a mark.

If you're near it, run away
Or you will pay.
He's getting his own back on you
For all the things you put him through.

Like you cooked his mum and dad
Which made him very mad.

He's going to eat you all
Even if you are small or tall.

Tom Best (11)
Leeds Grammar School

THE SNOWBALL FIGHT

I can see snow with my sight
I'm off to have a snowball fight
Put my socks on nice and tight
I will have to use all my might
For there nearly comes the dreadful night.

Hope I don't get chilly
Because I'm sometimes silly.
So I'm off to play in new snow
I can't wait to go
So I can whitewash my friend Joe
I'll put all my anger in my throw.

Keiron Garrity (10)
Leeds Grammar School

WORLD WAR II

It started in 1939
When Adolf Hitler, a frightful guy
Sent his army off to war,
To change England to the Nazi law.

The bombers flew to the largest towns
And dropped their great big bombs right down.
The result of the bombing was devastating
And the Germans were celebrating.

The children, the evacuees,
Were sent to Wales and the River Tees
Where the Germans didn't attack,
But that became their biggest lack.
For in the North and West Yorkshire
The people worked without tire,
To make the weapons to win the war
And destroy the Nazi law.

Jamie Morris (11)
Leeds Grammar School

PAUL

There was a man called Paul
And believe me, he looked as though he'd had a fall.
His trousers were all ripped,
His eyes popped out like pips.

His face was covered in gruesome scars
And he loved his flashy cars
And always gloated to his friends
And was never ready to lend.

Robert Nicholson (10)
Leeds Grammar School

TENNIS

Tennis, tennis, wonderful tennis,
They play this game from here to Venice.
Nothing can stop the flying ball,
Except the racket as it falls.

I hit the ball,
It goes up high,
If it hits you, you will squeal,
But if you're quick, it's as easy as pie.

You hit the smash,
It hits the ground.
You've really given it a good hard bash.
You've won the match
The crowd begin to cheer,
Now it's time for some beer.

Peter Fisher (11)
Leeds Grammar School

A POET INTERRUPTED

Looking through the window, this is what I see
Over by the wall, a bush and a tree.
When I look closer things appear
Like stones and rats and a rabbit's ear.
The more I look, the more I see
A cat, a dog, an apple in a pear tree.
Right on the window sill, underneath my nose
A bee buzzes loudly around a prickly rose.
Over on the path where the paving stones slant
An anteater sucks on a city of ants.
A plane roars overhead, I look up
Blast! I've spilt my coffee cup!

Adam Bergen (10)
Leeds Grammar School

ALICE AND HER MAGIC TOY BEAR

Alice bought a magic bear,
With fluffy, golden-brown hair.
Alice tucked him in her bed
But then a voice, here's what it said.

'Alice, I am a magic bear,
Just touch me on my gold-brown hair
And I will take you anywhere
Or give you such a frightful scare
It depends on the words you say, do you dare?'

Alice said the magic words
And she was flying with the birds.
She picked the right words to say
And she had fun all through the day.

After all that fun she had,
She never, ever told her dad.
And with the bear she says the words
And she is flying with the birds!

Sam Brown (10)
Leeds Grammar School

THE HOLIDAYS

Oh the joy of the holiday's arriving!
Relaxation, swimming and diving.
It is our much-needed break,
A trip to the beach,
Fishing in a lake,
Sipping an ice-cold lemonade,
In a rubber ring, as you wade,
Searing heat from the sun,
Makes you not want to run.
As you reach the end of Heaven,
Hours to boarding, only seven.
Tickets shown to the steward,
He rips them up, as if skewered.
Soaring away into the skies,
Any description would not be lies.
Indescribable it may be,
Views of the mountains, views of the sea.
Touchdown and it's all over,
Back to home, in our Rover.

David Franklin (11)
Leeds Grammar School

LEEDS UNITED

Leeds United is the team
To win the cup is their dream
The manager has lots of money
The players prefer to play when it's sunny.

There are eleven players who are eager to play
On that very special day.
The fans cheering, what a sound
Singing, shouting, it's just so loud.

The stadium is called Elland Road
The pitch is in great condition because it's been mowed
Their kit is blue, yellow and white
Manchester United are not so bright.

James Shippey (11)
Leeds Grammar School

AUTUMN

In autumn the leaves crackle up and die,
On the ground they form a sea of colour,
They are like an army, which has dropped
From the sky.

The days start to get shorter and
The nights start to get longer
The harvest is taken in at the start
Of the season.

The season of autumn is
The most colourful season of the year.
The season of autumn is a time of
Work and a fresh start at school.

Alex Davidson (11)
Leeds Grammar School

WINTER

This is the one that starts the year off; yes, winter is season number one.
The days get shorter and nights get longer and colder
And the longer and hotter days of summer and autumn have gone.

Winter is a season of which there are festivals and loads of fun.
But while playing in the snow and unwrapping our presents,
We are all deep down missing the summer sun.

Winter is a time of celebrating, when we celebrate the years gone by us.
But while we are snug in our houses,
The robin is not quite so fortuitous.

The Jewish people celebrate Hanukkah, and this can be called
The Festival of Lights.
But at this time in the Christian religion, they have Santa Claus right in
their sights.

The Christian people then celebrate Christmas, with decorations,
Dinners and religious services.
But on the religious side of this time, they celebrate the birth of Jesus.

After all of these festivals there is just one more to enjoy,
The beginning of the new year, that is celebrated with
extravagance and joy.

It is celebrated with, for example, firework displays,
But also in many other ways.

Meanwhile in the animal world, the last of the birds are migrating.
But the animals not able to fly, are on the ground curled up,
hibernating.
The animals can't gather any more food in the night or day,
Because the thick, crispy, white blanket of snow is in their way.

The children are building snowmen and having snowball fights,
But though they think they're having fun,
They should just be waiting for the worst weather to come.

Haydon Davidson (10)
Leeds Grammar School

I WISH I WAS FUNNY

I really wish I was funny,
Then everyone would be my friend,
So I've tried telling jokes but they say,
I've driven them round the bend.

I really want to be funny,
But now I'm in despair,
I've even tried looking stupid,
But they just stand and stare.

I've really tried to be funny,
But comedy's not in my blood,
Every time I open my mouth,
They shove my head in mud.

I really wish I was funny,
So I could hear their applause,
But when I'm supposed to hear laughter,
The only noise I hear is their snores.

Joe Watson (11)
Leeds Grammar School

MY HAMSTER

I have a little hamster,
A gift he was to me.
All my family hate him,
He has one eye you see.

Cyclops is the name I call him,
People think he's weird.
But I just like him anyway,
'Cause he's too little to be feared.

My mum says I can have another pet,
To play with and adore.
Perhaps a little rabbit,
To scurry around the floor.

Her offer is so very kind,
To have another pet.
But Cyclops is so unique,
I don't want to swap him . . . yet.

Joe Wallen (11)
Leeds Grammar School

WHY CAN'T CHILDREN BE LIKE ADULTS?

Why can't children be like adults,
Partying and staying up late?
Instead, *we* go to bed early,
Usually earlier than eight!

Why can't children be like adults,
Choosing what they eat?
Instead *we* have no choice in this,
It's veg, potato and meat!

Why can't children be like adults,
Making their own decision?
I can't wait till I'm old enough,
Not to ask permission!

Why can't children be like adults?
They don't have to go to schools!
We have to study long and hard
And follow all the rules!

Why can't children be like adults,
Paying all the bills?
Wait a minute, that's not good,
I think I'll stick with childhood and its thrills!

Rudy Harris (10)
Leeds Grammar School

FOOTBALL

Shirt in the airing cupboard
Shin pads smelly but hard.
Shorts crinkled, mucky and tattered
My mum was really shattered
After washing my mucky mess.

The day of the match
Wasn't really up to scratch.
The rain poured fast and hard,
Although we all brought umbrellas
They didn't really keep us
From getting wet and damp.

I'm running up the pitch
Really, really wanting to ditch
The defending player beside me.
I am passed the ball
I shoot at the goal
I really want to score.

The crowd's silent and still
They watch as the ball
Soars into the wide goalmouth
And the crowd goes wild
'Goal!' they all shout, 'goal!'

Russell Heatley (10)
Leeds Grammar School

THE LIFE OF JAMES BOND

Have you ever wondered how James Bond came to be how he is?
Have you ever wondered how he got his phrases?
Have you ever wondered how he became so sneaky?

It goes back to his childhood,
When he was young and smaller then,
His dad could have been an agent,
So that would have influenced him,
He probably went round with popgun in hand.
You can imagine him at register time at school,
The teacher shouting, 'Bond?'
And he would reply, 'James Bond.'
Hanging around with Alec and M
And Q, trying to make a special pen or something.

He grew up to join M16 like his dad,
With a mission from M and gadgets from Q,
He's got a license to kill
And he gets all the girls,
'The name's Bond, James Bond.'

Thomas Papworth-Smith (10)
Leeds Grammar School

The Seasons Of Life

Spring is a baby who bounds into life,
Innocent, unknowing and new.
The bulb and the leaf unfurl in the light
And drink in the fresh morning dew.

In *summer* the child who plays without cares,
Is maturing, growing and learning.
The trees and the plants grow longer and stronger,
Sun ripening the fruits they are bearing.

The adult of *autumn* in the prime of life,
Family, house, job and the holiday trip.
The colour starts fading, the leaves lose their hold,
The birds fly south, escaping winter's cold grip.

Illness and ageing are winter's cruel curse,
As the body decays towards death.
But *winter* is a pause in the circle of life,
Before the spring brings new shoots up afresh.

Jacob Francis Ehrlich (10)
Leeds Grammar School

WAVES

There are big waves and little waves
Green waves and blue
Waves you can jump over
Waves you dive through.

Waves that rise up
Like a great water wall
Waves that swell softly
And don't break at all.

Waves that can whisper
Waves that can roar
And tiny waves that run at you
Running on the shore.

Thomas Pettican (10)
Leeds Grammar School

JAMES BOND

The name's Bond, James Bond,
Of spying and espionage I'm very fond.
I shoot to kill,
All women I thrill.
I travel a lot,
To get a clear shot,
At the latest villain on the scene,
I work for country and Queen.
I get gadgets from Q,
All my cars are stylish and new,
And when things go rather absurd,
I have a vodka martini - shaken, not stirred.

Alex Watson (11)
Leeds Grammar School

THE FIGHT

His eyes were like ice as he crossed the arena,
The other person looked like a ballerina.
Jumping up and down like a fool,
I'm sure if you looked, you'd think he was a ghoul.

Those eyes were flaming, his body was set,
It looked like he was in the team set.
Turning around he saw the opponent,
Flipped around and caught him like a component.

I'm sure if you saw him you'd think he was fake,
And after all that, I've got a confession to make,
That certain somebody was Sir Francis Drake!

Duncan Hallam (10)
Leeds Grammar School

THE OCEAN

As the ocean waves break
against the shore, the sun rises
from the horizon once more.

Fishing boats, liners,
yachts and tug boats,
all upon the sea they float.

The ocean is home to sharks,
seals, whales and fish,
some end up as a tasty dish.

Pacific, Atlantic, Black Sea and Red Sea,
not forgetting the good old Med,
that's how wonderful the ocean is.

Marco Sarussi (11)
Leeds Grammar School

CHARLIE

My friend Charlie loves coming to stay.
His eyes twinkle like stars,
His face splits into a big smile,
Showing me rows of pearl-white teeth.
He dances and prances around me
And makes me feel dizzy.

My friend Charlie loves coming to stay.
We play ball on the lawn all day.
As he runs up and down his black coat ripples in the wind
And he proudly wags his big feathery tail.
He clutches the ball between black leathery lips.
He drops it then laughs at me with his pink lollopy tongue.

My friend Charlie loves coming to stay.
When he's had his dinner he flops down by the stove.
He dreams of running through the fields
And his pink paws twitch in his sleep.
He sees a rabbit and his ears prick up.
Deep in his sleep he makes excited woofing noises.

Charlie is my best friend,
Charlie is my dog.

Jonathan Letts (10)
Leeds Grammar School

THE FEARFUL CHASE!

It could have happened morning, evening or night,
But it had to happen now; it hit him with fright,
The terror grew within him
The lights began to dim,
But he would not let his parents succeed, not without a fight!

He ran up the stairs, through every room and down the hallway
Behind the banister silently hiding, waiting for the next day,
The parents gave in and quietly slept,
But the job to be done, in their mind was kept,
But he would not give in if he were running till May!

His parents were sleeping, silently sleeping,
They were not at all opening their eyes or peeping,
So the boy crept downstairs,
Took from the fridge and went back upstairs,
While his parents were still sleeping, silently sleeping without peeping!

Then, so quickly, his parents jumped out of bed,
The boy ran to his room, all painted red,
He firmly locked the door
And he tried to ignore,
The great feeling of fear right at the back of his head.

Then his door began to terribly, terribly shake
And the boy was scared and began to quake,
His parents rammed into the door,
Several splinters fell on the floor,
The door fell down to reveal his parents, both thin as a rake!

His parents grabbed him; they had done the math,
The boy fell down to the floor, he fell to their wrath,
The moment he had feared had arrived,
He wished he had run or maybe dived,
But he had to face a terrible fate, yes he had to have a bath!

Robert Morgan (11)
Leeds Grammar School

THE SNAKE

I love the snake
I love the way it slithers
And stirs.

I love the snake
I love its shiny
White fangs that
Dig deep into flesh
And prey.

I love the snake
I love the curvy
Marks on the ground
That make it untraceable
To predators around.

I love the snake
I love its beady
Little yellow eyes
And the slit of purple
Which makes it evil
And sly!

Luke Mirzabaigian (10)
Leeds Grammar School

THE MOUNTAIN

High in the sky,
The ice-capped peak reaches for the sun;
Impossible to conquer,
Proud and fearless.

Down in the valley,
The climber waits;
As small as an ant,
The climber is scared.

Looking up,
He sees the sky;
The mountain's still so thick,
A long way to climb, thought he.

A mile or two it looked
Shining down,
So snowy and slippy it looks,
Just half a mile up;

It's only a mountain,
The climber thought,
With two miles to go,
It isn't.

The climber set off,
Scared and all,
He just had to keep calm,
For he was shaking already.

Sam Grant (10)
Leeds Grammar School

THE BATTLEFIELD

A thousand bodies on the ground,
A silent world, not a sound.
A black flag waves in the air,
Then comes a knight, mounted on mare.

He rode through the bodies without a breath,
His name was Doom, his name was Death.
He looked at the bodies without trouble or strife,
The destroyer of mothers, the destroyer of life.

But then on the field he found,
A live man writhing on the ground
Death took out his darkened spear
And started to come ever near.

The man looked up to the sky.
Death was coming, Death was nigh.
Then out came the man's blade
And into the body of Death it laid.

The man rose up, he had won,
Down came the darkness, out came the sun.
This story shall forever yield,
This is the story of the battlefield.

William Lord (10)
Leeds Grammar School

A LITTLE MONKEY

As I was walking down the street,
A stubborn man I came to meet.
He had a table made of wood
And on this table there it stood.
A little monkey filled with rage
Was locked inside a metal cage.

It jumped around and banged the bars
And shouted and screamed at passing cars.
It looked at me with eyes of red and
Picked up its fruit and aimed at my head.
It flew through the air and hit with a *splat*
I shouted out, 'You little brat!'

The man turned round and with disgrace
Lifted the monkey up, face to face.
The monkey coughed a little burp.
The man shouted, 'You stupid twerp!'
I thought that he was cool and funky
But he is bad, that little monkey.

Matthew McGoldrick (11)
Leeds Grammar School

MY RABBIT

My rabbit is called Sooty
He is actually very cute
He is a Netherland Dwarf
That makes him minute.

He strolls about the house
One would think he's a king
And he knows where to go
When he needs the ting-a-ling.

He watches Coronation Street
Lying in front of the fire
Sitting there with his nose in the air
With the heat at his feet.

He loves green beans
Carrots are a *no*
Munching and guzzling from his own bowl
He is the best pet so he will *never* go.

Michael Ballmann (11)
Leeds Grammar School

SNOWBOUND

I like winter,
The fire in the grate,
Lamps lit,
Maybe the promise of snow.

The wind bellows,
The chimney roars,
Red logs burn and crackle,
Safe and comfortable we sit.

Snow piled high,
A perfect white blanket,
A snowman to build,
Snowballs to throw.

Christmas memories are still warm,
The light is flooding back,
A robin sings to the winter sky,
Snowdrops are uncovered.

James Leftley (11)
Leeds Grammar School

THE SHIP IN A STORM

The air was fresh with a mild blow
The ship was ready to leave the harbour
The engines on the Prince started to roar
The smell of fumes came with a gust of wind.

The crew stopped the ship and we lowered the anchor and nets
Once again the creak of the rusted winch lowered the chains
Into the sea.
In six hours we will be going home to sit in front of the fire
And watch TV
Suddenly there was a shout from the bridge, 'Raise the nets,
Raise the anchor; serious storm coming our way. All hands on deck.'

It took us ten minutes to raise both the anchor and the nets
But it was too late. The storm had already hit us;
Waves were rising ten, maybe twenty, feet in the air.
I shouted, 'Abandon ship.' Everyone jumped into the sea.
It was freezing cold. We all swam towards the shore but only I made it.

Fraser Dunlop (11)
Leeds Grammar School

POETRY COMPETITION

There was an old lady from Fife
And all she held was a knife
In less than an hour
She had all the power
To rule the kingdom of Fife.

Sean Longthorpe (10)
Manston St James Primary School

AN ALPHABETICAL POEM

For this class I give to you
Here is a list of all their names
And what they have and like:

A   is for Andy who is handy,
B   is for Ben who eats candy.
C   is for Callum that has two pet mice,
D   is for Dean who plays games with a dice.
E   is for Eric who likes school,
F   is for Fred who thinks he's cool.
G   is for George who loves to go on beaches,
H   is for Harry who is afraid of leeches.
I   is for Irene who screams when she sees rats,
J   is for Jack who loves cats.
K   is for Kenny who always fights,
L   is for Linda who flies kites.
M is for Mandy, won't stop tying knots,
N   is for Nicholas that loves dot-to-dots.
O   is for Olivia, crushes ants,
P   is for Peter that doesn't ever change his pants.
Q   is for Quentin who cleans with a mop,
R   is for Ryan who wears a Leeds United top.
S   is for Sam that eats baked beans,
T   is for Timmy who blames things on Dean.
U   is for Ursula whose mum is a teacher,
V   is for Venus whose dad is a preacher.
W is for William who wears gel in his hair,
X   is Xavier that goes to bed with a teddy bear.
Y   is for Yolanda whose dad has a Land Rover,
Z   is for Zac that has loads of four-leaf clovers.

Now that this class is yours
I shall watch you as your tears pour!

Jack Walker (11)
Manston St James Primary School

Box

In my room is a box
How boring is that?
It's a brown rectangle,
Fancy that!

My box is a train
No bus! No car!
Whatever I pretend
I don't get far.

My box is empty
There's nothing to see
Oh just one thing,
A little dead flea.

The box has gone
The dog's got it
She having puppies
It will be chewed to bits.

The box is gone
For evermore
The pups chewed it
That's for sure.

I've got a new box
Who cares anyway!
It's just a bit of cardboard
I've got puppies to play!

Bethany Pryor (10)
Manston St James Primary School

THE FOREST

The grass snake is moving, moving with ease
Among the twigs and grass and leaves,
He's hissing and twisting and coiling and spitting.

Among the bracken and frosty wood,
The wolf, she is prowling and is up to no good.
She's growling and howling and creeping and sniffing.

Among the deep and rich, rich soil,
The mole is descending, his blood at the boil.
He's digging and ploughing and shovelling and burrowing.

Soaring and soaring, on this autumn night,
The owl is hunting with crystal clear sight.
She's hooting and swooping and snatching and catching.

The toad is jumping around the oak,
Out of its mouth comes a feeble croak.
He's croaking and leaping and pulsing and swimming.

Out from a hole, finished laying her eggs,
Crawls a black widow, with long, slender legs.
She's spying and crawling and scuttling and biting.

A flash of black claws and thick, matted hair,
From the depths of the forest comes the grizzly bear.
He's lumbering and clawing and slashing and roaring.

Standing strong and tall, roots firm in the ground,
The tree's falling leaves make a delicate sound.
It's rustling and creaking and swaying and whipping.

The spirit of the forest, the entity of the world,
The wind was singing, round my body she twirled.
She's whistling and humming and whooshing and swirling.

The spirits of the forest were all mentioned here,
But because of mankind,
They will soon disappear . . .

Joseph Kerry (11)
Manston St James Primary School

THE BEAST

Deep in the forest,
There is a dark cave,
Where the beast has his nest!

Nothing can stop this beast!
Every night he bounds to the village
And has a massive feast!

The villagers thought,
What can we do?
They sat for days,
And finally they called up
Sir Lou!

He eventually came,
But never did he,
Expect that he would
Have to conquer thee!

That was the end of poor Sir Lou,
But at least he had done his job,
For never did the beast return,
With his beastly crew!

Matthew Wise (10)
Manston St James Primary School

WHAT AM I?

Day by day,
By the river it lay.
They can be big,
They can be small.

Day by day,
By the river it lay,
They can be patterned,
They can be plain.

Day by day,
By the river it lay.
They can be round,
They can be square.

Day by day,
By the river it lay,
They can crumble,
They make us tumble.

Robyn Ward (11)
Manston St James Primary School

DOLPHIN

A graceful creature,
As quick as a bullet,
Shooting across the ocean,
Making no sound but clicks and whistles,
The sunlight glitters on its silver-grey body,
Suddenly it explodes out of the water's surface so quickly,
Then . . .
Splash, back down.

Courtney Parr (11)
Manston St James Primary School

THE RIVER TELLS ITS STORY

Stony on the bottom,
Sparkly at the top,
Cutting valleys along the way,
Rivers flowing on and on.

Water coming to its mouth,
Getting colder along the way,
Fresh, deep water, twinkling,
Now it's soft, calm, gentle.

Transparent, it's so clean,
Now it's going through a viaduct,
It gives off life, the lovely stuff,
Nothing can describe it at all.

Water! Water! Down the river,
Sometimes it makes me shiver.

You can hear it if you listen,
Touch it, feel it, don't be scared,
Safely swimming in the river,
Now you'll see it's a splashing good day.

Kayleigh Schietaert (9)
Micklefield CE Primary School

THE RAIN AND SEA

The rain is wet.
The rain will wet you.
The sea is freezing.
The sea has big waves.
The rain sploshes and splashes.
The rain hits your umbrella.
The sea crashes down.

Kieran Martin-Rushworth (7)
Micklefield CE Primary School

WATER

Water, water, can be rain.
Water, water can be twinkling and trickling down mountains.
It can flow down rivers.
Water can be clean or dirty.
Under the water can be rocky, sandy and soft.
Water, water, can be so icy that you can slip.
Water, water, overflows.
Water, water, can fall down as a waterfall.
Water, water, can pitter-patter!

Jessica Kidd (8)
Micklefield CE Primary School

WATER, WATER

Water, water, is smooth
Water, water, is on the move
Water, water, is so cool
Water, water, goes into the pool.
Water, water, like the rain.
Water, water, is a pain.
Water, water, in a river.
Water, water, makes me shiver.
Water, water, in the lake,
Water, water, makes me shake.

Joshua Eyles (8)
Micklefield CE Primary School

BEAUTIFUL LAKE WATER

Lake water,
Lake water,
The deep, freezing lake water.
Never boiling, always freezing,
But still and very calm,
Always safe, sometimes rough,
The curving, swirling water,
Starts off very calm,
And after a while it gets rough.
The relaxing lake water,
The calm lake water,
The rippling lake water
Is such a beautiful sight.
It sometimes is bubbly,
And sometimes not,
Lake water,
Lake water,
Such a beautiful sight!

Ashleigh Roberts (9)
Micklefield CE Primary School

THE RAIN

The rain stops, it is sometimes slippy,
Then it starts to get nippy.
Most of the time the rain gets icy,
Also it sometimes seems shiny,
The rain is calm and sometimes looks blue,
Now I have got the flu.
Still the rain is sloppy,
Now it is getting rocky!

Emma Stanley (8)
Micklefield CE Primary School

SEAWATER

The seawater, seawater,
delicate blue, dazzling water.
The smooth, safe, sparkling water.
Dripping, sloppy waves
whirling in the sea,
smashing water onto the cliffs.
Dirty, sometimes clean,
meandering, curving sea.
Swishing, curving sea,
swishing, smashing water.
Some seas hot, some seas cold,
cold, warm, it's all the same.
Curve, curve, let's see.
Drip-drop, drip-drop.

Elizabeth Grace (7)
Micklefield CE Primary School

WATER

The water is safe.
The water is fast.
The water is still.
The water is blue.
The water is see-through.
The water is dazzling.
The water is sinking.
The water is dripping.
The water is shining.
The water is sloppy.

Thomas McNally (7)
Micklefield CE Primary School

THE RAIN

The wonderful see-through rain, it twinkles on your head.
The dazzling blue rain, it's sloppy on your head.
The slippy rain, it drenches your clothes.
The fast rain makes puddles on the ground.
The pitter-patter rain, it makes so much noise.
The fast blue rain, it hurts your head.
The slimy rain, it is so dirty.
The relaxing rain, it is so nice.
The splashing rain, it splatters on your head.

Lewis Parker (9)
Micklefield CE Primary School

THE FLOOD

A flood of sparkling water
A flood of icy-cold water
A flood of thundering waterfalls
A fast, furious flood
A calm, gigantic flood
The shimmering, deep flood
The water meandering
The water is powerful
The waves splash against the rocks.

Johnny Smith (9)
Micklefield CE Primary School

LISTEN TO THE SEA

S h h h h h h h h h
   h h h h h h h h h h h!

    still,   still,
Sit   very

And . . . listen.

                  to   sea.

          Listen   the

         Stroking   sand.
               the

       on   to   beachcomber
Whispers   high the   trees.

  Sit . . . still,

  And . . . listen!

Holly Nicholson (9)
Micklefield CE Primary School

WATER

Crashing, bashing, in the sea catching fishes for my tea.
Water's running very fast, has *no* air to stop at last.
Water, water, go right down, water, water, don't go round.
Water floods down the stream, merrily, merrily, quite a dream.
The lake is nice, the lake is blue, you don't know what you can do.
Water's slow, water's fast and it can never last.
River's fun, water's fun, nothing's fun without a bun!

Magan Davies (8)
Micklefield CE Primary School

WATER RHYME

Water, water, ru   down the drain
           nn
             ing

Water, water, it co   be rain.
            ul
             d

Water, water, sl   and *cr*
         as   *as*
          hi   *hi*
           ng   *ng*

Water, water, sw   and *cu*
       ir   *li*   *rl*   *in*
        ng   *g*

Water, water, s p a r k l i n g blue
Water, water, it's b e t t e r if it's new.

Water, water, in a p u d d l e
Water, water, never gets in a m u d d l e.

Water, water, is really i c y
Water, water, never gets s l i c y.

Kelly Stracey (9)
Micklefield CE Primary School

THE BULL

A bull ready to charge at me stares at me
Glares at me with its red devil eyes.

It is like a dark night
Its body is as rough as sandpaper.
Its horns are as bright as a light.
The gold ring through its nose is as shiny as a wedding ring.

The bull's feet are like scooping the cream from the floor
When it stamps its feet.
The bull rocking side to side like a see-saw
Charging at me, glaring at me.

Guy Yeadon (10)
Ninelands Primary School

IF . . .

If you can face up to your fears
If you can stare them in the eyes
If you can get over stage fright.

If you can sing out
If you cannot be sick before you go on
If you can be rejected but never give up
You'll be a star!

Ashleigh Berry (9)
Ninelands Primary School

THE MAGIC BOX
(Based on 'Magic Box' by Kit Wright)

I will put in the box . . .

The furious flapping of a tropical toucan
a cruel cackle from an earthquake
the burning feel of the bulging sun.

I will put in the box . . .

All the nine planets orbiting the sun
the clutching, cold, coral Atlantic
a dragon's flame hotter than a volcano.

I will put in the box . . .

A piece of shiny silver surface from the moon
and the North Star bright and big.

My box is fashioned with stars and planets
gold hinges are the sun's rays
and the handles are made out of the Earth's core.

I'll explore my box and see everything in it.

Conor Howard (11)
Ninelands Primary School

WHO DO YOU THINK YOU ARE?

I'm a booming gong being very loud!
I am a cold breeze breathing down everyone's necks.
I am a car driving my mum round the bend.
I am a football fan.
I am a grizzly, grumpy bear hating being woken up in the morning.
I am a light bulb full of energy!

Daniel Davison (9)
Ninelands Primary School

Haiku Poems

Holly Wreaths

Frosty holly leaves,
Hang on wreaths at people's doors.
Carol-singers sing.

Sparkling Snow

Sparkling snow falls down,
Covering the country fields.
Let's go out and play.

Feeling Comfy

Sitting on my chair,
Drinking cocoa by the fire,
Feeling comfortable.

Katie Williams (8)
Ninelands Primary School

If . . .

If you can walk on a beam without falling off,
If you can cartwheel on a bench with not one limb out of line,
If you can do the splits as straight as a line,
If you can go over the vault without your legs looking like
                                    a donkey's back legs,
If you can do an upward circle and keep your hips at the bar,
If you can hold dish shape for more than a minute,
Then you are a super gymnast!

Alexandra Falkingham (9)
Ninelands Primary School

THE MAGIC BOX
(Based on 'Magic Box' by Kit Wright)

I will put in the box . . .

The twittering of a tropical toucan
The spells of an old wicked witch
And the sound of a horrible angry dragon.

I will put in the box . . .

The cry of a princess waiting for her prince
And the song of the sweetest bird.

I will put in the box . . .

The sounds of the rainforest
The riches and fortunes of the world
And the football skills of David Beckham.

I will put in the box . . .

A sunset on the horizon
The wonders of the world
And the sands of time rushing away.

My box is the best box in the world
Made with gold and silver
With planets on the lid and magic in the corners.

I will sunbathe in my box
On a beautiful sunshine-yellow beach
Then I will sail far, far away.

Rebecca Louise Roddy (10)
Ninelands Primary School

CHEER UP SONG

No one likes a boaster
And I'm not one to boast,
But everyone who knows me
Knows that I'm the most!
Everyone says I'm the number one reader,
Animals love me because I'm the best feeder,
I'm Einstein's big brain inside his small head,
I exercise all day, even in bed,
Jeremy Strong's stories are as good as mine,
Everybody says my stories are fine,
I'd win the best book contest.
At nearly everything I'm the best.
Who is the most intelligent?
Me! Me! Me!

Daniel Cale (9)
Ninelands Primary School

LION

My lion is fighting flawlessly on a cliff
With the ocean down and the sky up.
Roaring, charging, fighting.
As quick as a flash he sprints towards his prey.
Stealthily and powerfully he charges
Then prowls,
　　　　　　　proudly
　　　　　　　　　　　away!

Callum Massey (11)
Ninelands Primary School

WHO DO YOU THINK YOU ARE?

I'm a speedy cheetah, fast and furious,
I'm a monkey swinging among trees,
I'm a locked door holding secrets inside,
I'm a never-worn suit, clean and shiny,
I'm a spear whenever I'm made mad,
I'm a grumpy elephant when I'm walking around a supermarket,
I'm a star brightening up everybody's life!

Daniel Kershaw (10)
Ninelands Primary School

MY FRIEND

My friend and I have a bond,
So strong, we will never part,
My friend and I have a bond
So strong we will always play,
My friend and I have a bond,
So strong we will never fight,
My friend and I have a bond
So strong we will never part.

Daniel Fearnley (8)
Ninelands Primary School

WHO DO YOU THINK YOU ARE?

I am a shuttlecock flying across the court
I am a light shining on everybody's face and watching them glow
I am an early bird waking up in the azure sky
I am a jukebox singing to every song
I am a sealed envelope because I never tell secrets.

Olivia Hawley (10)
Ninelands Primary School

MY FRIEND

My friend likes to fight,
He does this day and night,
My friend calls me a liar,
We get on like a house on fire,
My friend's a tiny bit grumpy
But when he's silly he's really funny,
Although he teases me a bit
He's really my best friend.
My friendship towards him
Will never end!

Charlotte Mather (8)
Ninelands Primary School

WHAT IS RED?

Chapped lips as the cold wind goes by
Poppies swaying in the distant sunset
Gurgling blood and stained wire
Rosy cheeks of lost loved ones
The crimson rims of tired eyes that can't be kept open
Gunfire causing blood to leak from the body
The anger of the soldiers as they watch their fellow men die
Innocent humans losing their lives.

Bethany Fox (10)
Ninelands Primary School

MY DOG

The dog
Sniffing the
roses with his black nose
and big brown eyes.
His fluffy white coat is as
white as a snowman,
his mouth cracks and his
tail waggles as he wants to play.

Hello doggy!

James Goodall (10)
Ninelands Primary School

MY DOG

As white as the clouds.
Likes the long, lush, grassy, green field.
He runs rapidly, racing up and down,
Bouncing and jumping up to his huge, yellow ball.
Rolling around, up and down,
Tossing and turning, boldly he leaps and barks
Excitedly in the summer sun.

Woof! Grrrrr!

Luke Quarmby (10)
Ninelands Primary School

WHEN I WAS ON THE SLIDER

When I was on the slider,
I didn't know what to do,
I started to feel giddy,
I went really fast too,

When I was on the slider,
I went round a big bed,
I thought I would fall over,
But I didn't, I reached the end,

When I was on the slider,
I went shooting into the pool,
I landed on a swimmer,
Who shouted, 'What a fool!'

Elliott Habgood (9)
Richmond House School

HELLO STRANGER

Hello Stranger, it's been too long,
I don't see your face in the mirror,
So I weep with tears and sorrow
And hope you'll be back tomorrow.
It's been months now but it seems like years,
There have been a few tears
But I've got right through to the end.

Hello Stranger,
You're a stranger no more.
Now I see your face coming through my door.

Connie July (9)
Richmond House School

IF I WAS A FOOTBALLER

If I was a footballer,
I was the captain of my team,
I scored loads of goals,
But only in last night's dream.

Then one day I got injured
And finally I got a long rest,
Two weeks later I was OK,
The time had come to play Arsenal with Henry, that pest!

Then one day I played for England
And we scored eight goals
And disappointingly I got a yellow card,
Eventually the next day came and I fell down the toilet hole.

Rajvir Dutt (10)
Richmond House School

HERE ARE THE ARMS

Here are the arms that should not have touched something,
Here are the eyes that saw something coming,
Here are the legs that went like a rocket,
Here is the tummy wanting baloney,
Here is the mouth eating as quickly as it can,
Here are the ears hearing the raise of a hand,
Here is the bum going red from the hand,
Here is the brain getting a message,
Here are the eyes again seeing stars
Then that reminded me never to touch that vase.

Alex Payne (10)
Richmond House School

MY SISTER

My sister's the one I hate,
She thinks she's good at squash
She runs around madly
Trying to act posh.

Her friends think she's nice
And also rather fun
But I personally think
She's got a big fat bum!

She's got lots of boyfriends
And goes on lots of dates
Once she walked through her boyfriend's gates
And then got drunk with all her mates.

When I stole the mansion's mail
The alarms began to wail
The CCTV tried to catch me on tape
Luckily, I was wearing an invisibility cape!

Oliver Penn (9)
Richmond House School

WHEN I WAS ON THE UNDERGROUND

When I was on the underground
It really was a pain
By the time I got to the airport
I'd already missed my plane.

When I was on the underground again
It really was a pain
When I got to the airport
I shouted, 'I've missed my plane to Spain!'

Alexandra Sargeant (10)
Richmond House School

I'D LIKE TO BE A PEA

I'd like to be a pea,
I'd always get flicked around,
I'd play hide-and-seek with the chips
And hide with the burger until we were found.

I'd have a ride on the fork,
Into outer space,
Then when I get to the top
I'd dive into the table's face.

Then one day my wish came true,
When I woke up in bed,
I was really scared
Because I was smaller than my own head.

Then came my sister,
She knocked me off the bed,
Then came her foot,
Then I was dead.

Now I'm a ghost,
No one can see me,
For I am cool,
I am a mushy pea.

Jeremy Ramsden (9)
Richmond House School

WHEN I WAS IN MY BEDROOM

When I was in my bedroom
Getting into bed
I heard a knock on the door
And I felt a bang on my head.

I looked up all around me
And amazingly I saw
A big, green, slimy monster
Waiting at the door.

The monster walked around a bit
Looking at the ground
I wondered what he was doing
Moving slowly around.

I walked straight towards him
I wasn't very scared
He looked at me with big yellow eyes
And just stared and stared and stared.

Eventually I noticed
He was mumbling in Spanish
And in two ticks
He absolutely vanished.

Julia H Shaw (9)
Richmond House School

WHEN I WAS ON THE PIER

When I was on the pier,
Leaning against the bin,
Suddenly it wobbled
And it and I fell in.

Now I'm in the water
And I'm frightened to death,
I was really afraid that
I'd sink into the depths.

Sharks underneath me,
Swimming around,
I accelerated at the speed of light,
To get to safe ground.

As soon as I got to the beach,
I raced to the shop,
I bought something secret
And two cans of pop.

Now I'm on the pier,
With my friend too,
Leaning against the bin,
Which is stuck with superglue.

'The only bad thing now,'
I said to my friend, really snappy,
'Is that the poor bin men
Are not going to be happy.'

Ben Balmforth (10)
Richmond House School

I AM THE FOUR SWORD

I am
The Four Sword
And I have
Seen battles
And wars.

Heroes have
Drawn me
From the
Scabbard
And I
Cut down
Their foes.

My name
Comes from
The power
I hold
In my
Blade.

A hero
In danger
Shall be
Cloned
As four
A great war
Has been
Split in four.

I have been
Sealed in
A chamber
In a stone
I stay
If you draw me
I'll
Serve you
Well.

Ben Perren (9)
Richmond House School

THE WRITER OF THIS POEM

(Based on 'The Writer of this Poem' by Roger McGough)

The writer of this poem,
Is as clever as deep blue,
As deep thinking as Kasparov
And as sticky as glue.

As thin as a snake,
As fast as a fish,
As athletic as a monkey
And as hard as a dish.

I am very clever,
I'm as quick as a jiffy,
But I must admit,
This book's a bit whiffy.

Alexander Browne (9)
Richmond House School

WHAT I LIKE BEST

What I like best
Yes, most of all
In my whole life
Is kicking a ball
Kicking a ball
Kicking a ball
Not songs on the bus
Or hymns in the hall
Not running or rounders
But kicking a ball.

Second best, I think, after all
Will have to be
Hitting a ball
Keep your knitting
And your running
What I like second
Of all is hitting a ball
Hitting a ball
Hitting a ball
And that's what I like
Second of all.

Oliver Iles (9)
Richmond House School

THE MONSTER

The monster hides behind the cupboard,
but you can't see him there,
he jumps out when you're not watching,
so you better now beware.

The monster lurks under the bed,
waiting for you to pass by,
he very rarely misses a chance,
to freeze you with his evil eye.

The monster crouches behind the door,
ready to creep up on you
and if you dare to enter the room,
your chances will be very few.

Eleanor Gaffney (9)
Richmond House School

MY PET

My pet is cuddly and furry,
It's black and has a warm coat
So it could be a dog
Or could it be a horny goat?

My pet is orange and browny
And has small ears which are pink inside
So it could be a bunny
Or it couldn't because mine died.

My pet is brown and has horns,
It's mean and makes a noise like a puffalo
So it could be a deer
Or it could be a buffalo!

Sajid Mir (9)
Richmond House School

SHOPS

I love to shop
At Tammy and Pineapple,
I love to shop
At Top Shop and Jade.

I wish I could have
All the shops in the world
To have and to hold
Forever and ever.

How about a T-shirt?
What's wrong with some trousers
And a few blouses?
I never get tired
Of spending my money
It's better than chocolate
And sweeter than honey.

I go on and on
Can't seem to stop
I think I will always
Shop till I drop!

Emma Moran (10)
Richmond House School

THE SISTER

The sister was sly and secretive
Even though she had no secrets.
The sister was unkind at times, maybe nice at some.

The sister was walking home one day,
When into sight came her arch enemy since nursery!
Silica Smonzer.

At once they both put on brave faces,
As they walked by each other.
Silica whispered something to the sister.

The sister asked what she said.
Silica said, 'Will you be my friend?'
The sister said, 'Of course I will be your friend.'

And so they both became sly and secretive together,
Even though they both had no secrets.

Haleema Nadir (10)
Richmond House School

ANIMALS

A nts march in one straight line,
N ightingales sing their song!
I   mpalas jump up and down,
M onkeys swing from tree to tree,
A lligators have big smiles,
L eopards with their golden spots,
S harks swim on the ocean floor.

Bethany Wright (10)
Richmond House School

BUT WHY DOES A COW GO MOO?

Gorillas eat grapes on the ground,
Baboons eat bananas in the Bahamas
    But why does a cow go moo?

Butterflies flutter by my window
Grasshoppers gracefully grip the ground
Earwigs' ears drop on elves
    But why does a cow go moo?

Mice use maces to win their races
Rats run around in rings
Chipmunks chatter in cherry trees
    But why does a cow go moo?

Armadillos sleep with rounded pillows
Hedgehogs head towards the highway
Aardvarks make the best of card sharks
    But why does a cow go moo?

But why?
But why?
But why does a cow go moo?

Joe Ingham (10)
Richmond House School

CONCISE HINTS FOR NEW STUDENTS

If you meet the school bully on your way to school,
give him your money *quick!*
(You may have met an enemy).

Do remember to shop until you drop the day before
you start your new school.
This means you will be a member of the cool group in no time.

Leave Teddy at home.
(Yes, I know he misses you).

On your first morning, don't confuse the geeks with the cool girls.
The geeks will never forgive you!

Do remember to bring a packed lunch.
(Be warned, school lunches are poison!).

It's alright to enter the classroom without knocking.
It's OK, the boys' room is no longer out of bounds.

If the teacher has confiscated something, try and catch her
swapping it for bubblegum with the PE teacher.
(Then you can tell the head).

On Parents' Evening, if one of the teachers tells your mum and dad
you have been naughty, don't burst into tears.
(Just make a note of the teacher's name, get your own back on
him/her later).

Practise answering back - the teachers will hate it.

Bring a football.

Jessica Kempner (10)
Richmond House School

Do Kangaroos Moo?

Carps
play harps on coral
Skates
like skating on water
Goldfish
are cold fish in winter
But why can't a kangaroo moo?

Poodles
have oodles of fun
Pekinese
don't bend their knees
Dachshunds
dash under the table
But why can't a kangaroo moo?

Starlings
are brave things
Blue tits
have blue tracksuits
Woodpeckers
sit on a double-decker
But why can't a kangaroo moo?

Nits
are the pits
Ladybirds
aren't really birds
Butterflies
flutter by
But why can't a kangaroo moo?

Oliver Packman (9)
Richmond House School

DRAGONS

Tuna
play trombones at home
Shrimps
shrivel up and turn into imps
But why don't dragons drive?

Labradors
love laboratories and fishing rods
Schnauzers
wear trousers all the time
But why don't dragons drive?

Budgies
bake buns with flower buds on
Parrots
eat rotten carrots
But why don't dragons drive?

Crickets
take tickets to see cricket
Snails'
slime feels like nails
But why don't dragons drive?

Why don't dragons?
Why don't dragons?
Why don't dragons drive?

Celia Helen Marker (9)
Richmond House School

SCOTTISH BEDS

Scottish beds, Scottish beds!
And very comfy too
They are of course haunted
By ghouls that go 'Woo!'

Scottish beds, lovely beds!
Full of beauty and warmth
With boingy springs just for you
Which give your dreams a chance to launch!

Scottish beds, warm beds!
And just at half-price!
Because our beds are just so cheap
You'll have money to gamble on dice!

Oliver Dixon (10)
Richmond House School

MY POETRY RHYTHMS

Viduka passed the ball to Smith
And Smithy passed it back
Viduka took a cracking shot
And hit it with a whack.

The ball went sailing through the air
It sailed at quite a pace
Dudek looked up to the sky
And prayed it would land in space.

The ball hit Dudek in the face
That sent him to the ground
He had a terrible nose bleed
The crowd made a gasping sound.

Ben Sweeting (9)
Richmond House School

A POEM TO BE SPOKEN SILENTLY

It was so quiet that I heard a fly buzzing in my ear,
it sounded like hundreds of people marching down the street.

It was so peaceful that I heard a woodlouse cautiously scuttling
across the room like a constant tap in my head.

It was so still that I heard the grass waving in the wind
like my mum and my dad waving goodbye to me.

It was so silent that I heard a mouse sniffing for its food
like my baby sister crying all night long.

It was so still that I felt a spider crawl down my leg
like my mum tickling me all day long.

It was so calm that I sensed someone's foot sinking in the mud
like someone sinking into the ground.

Charlie Fairbank (10)
Richmond House School

MY DOGS

I have three dogs called Margaux, Bruno and Nell
And sometimes they really give me hell.
Bruno has a pointy head and when I send him to bed
He growls at me a lot.
Margaux has a cut paw which scrapes along the floor
And I think it should be put in a pot.
Nell looks like chocolate but when she's put on a plate
She just doesn't seem to cut.
I don't know what you think but I think all my dogs are cool
And one day I might bring them into school.

William Harrison (8)
Richmond House School

NOCTURNAL BEASTS

Nocturnal beasts come out at night,
Ghosts and ghouls come out to fight,
The chilling night is frightening,
weird supernaturals come out to fright.

At the cemetery I hear the river,
A cold wind blows, I stand and shiver.
Shadows leap from behind the stones,
Ghostly characters shake my bones.

When all the kids are asleep,
The vampires come out to seek,
They scare all the children,
And threaten to kill them.

Edward Crocker (10)
Richmond House School

THE SEA

The sea, the sea
Whispers softly
How it calls to me
'I am lost.'

Waves whirl
Round and round
Seaweed swirls
Outward bound.

Crashes down
Like it's alive
Spins around
Never dies.

Lauren Parkin (11)
Richmond House School

MY FAVOURITE SPORT

My favourite sport is football,
It requires a lot of skill.
I prefer it to cricket,
It's absolutely brill!

My favourite sport is football,
It's great to score a goal.
I prefer it to hockey,
Just hitting a ball with a pole.

My favourite sport is football,
Especially when we win!
I prefer it to basketball,
Though I've got bruises on my shin!

My favourite sport is football,
There's nothing to compare!
I prefer it to absolutely everything,
Except, losing isn't fair.

Alex Smithies (11)
Richmond House School

SCHOOL

Railings surround it,
It's a daunting sight,
The huge stone building,
In the dim grey light.

When classrooms are bare,
Just teachers and books,
People could say,
'School really sucks!'

But at Richmond House,
A caring community,
From the cares of the world,
We have immunity.

An empty corridor,
As the big kids work,
At play time the cloakroom,
Is where they all lurk.

Railings surround it,
It's a daunting sight,
The huge stone building,
In the dim grey light.

James Martin (11)
Richmond House School

WHEN I WAS THREE

When I was three,
I only thought of me.

I never wanted to read,
Or do a good deed.

I had a little tricycle,
But I fancied a bicycle.

I tried to have a go,
But my mum shouted, 'No!'

I had a friend, Lee,
Who liked to play with me.

We used to sing
And play on the swing.

Now you can see,
That's enough of me!

Sarah Milne (11)
Richmond House School

A Poem To Speak Silently

When the atmosphere is quiet I hear
myself breathing
like the hissing of a snake.

When the atmosphere is peaceful I see
the changing of the traffic lights
like the flashing of the sun when a cloud goes in front.

When the atmosphere is still I see
the swaying of the lamp posts
like the leaves on the bushes.

When the atmosphere is silent I see
the movement of an owl's wing
like the moving of the wind.

When the atmosphere is still I feel
a tree grow
like it was fast-forwarding.

When the atmosphere is calm I sense
the window steaming up
like when the kettle has just boiled.

When the atmosphere is quiet I hear
myself breathing
like the hissing of a snake.

Daniel Mercer (10)
Richmond House School

THE WEIRD FAMILY

There once was a family five,
Funny thing, they could all drive,
Drive people mad and up the wall!

The mother was called Diane,
She sizzled more than a frying pan.
She had a high laugh
But never took a bath.

The daughter was called Olive,
Her initials spelt out OIL,
She had a disgusting boil,
And her friends called her Olive Oil.

The father was called Father,
He smoked a lot
But he said he did not.

Grandparents were called Butter and Bread,
They're in the place that we all dread
So is the rest of the family,
They're in the 'Nut House' you see!

Natalie Donkin (11)
Richmond House School

THE LONE PINE TREE

On top of a rocky mountain,
Standing alone, a pine tree.
On a crisp, cold winter morning,
Snow, far as the eye could see.

An old woodcutter scrambled up,
His axe so heavy a load.
Felled the tree with three mighty blows,
Took it to his poor abode.

He took it in and stood it up,
Poor tree, so sad and afraid.
Children with decorations came,
With candles, tinsel and braid.

On Christmas morn, the tree stood proud,
Presents all scattered around.
Warmed with the glow of the bright fire,
A new family was found.

Rebecca Jones (10)
Richmond House School

MY SAD BROTHER

My sad brother has a big nose
Has fungus on his fat toes
Picks his nose while he's doing a pose
My sad brother has a big nose

My sad brother has a big nose
My sad brother has a big throat
He has such a nose, he's a toad
My sad brother has a big nose

My sad brother has a big nose
I want to kill him with his throat
My sad brother has a big butt
My sad brother has a big nose

My sad brother has a big nose
Has fungus on his fat toes
Picks his nose while he's doing a pose
My sad brother has a big nose.

Matthew Smith (11)
Richmond House School

SCHOOL, SCHOOL

School, school,
The place we go to work,
Teachers teaching, bells ringing
And my friends, David, John and Kirk.

Homework, homework
We get it every night,
Maths, fractions, English, spellings,
I never get them right.

Play time, play time,
The time we get to rest,
Balls flying, children screaming,
The time we get to run around before we do our tests.

School, school,
Is it all just one big rule?
Children learning, pens writing,
Why, oh why . . . do we have to go to school?

Joshua Habergham (11)
Richmond House School

CHRISTMAS PUDDING

Xmas pudding on the table,
Merry faces get the ladle,
All the terror and dread comes back,
Soon the cake will be attacked.

Pudding flying everywhere,
Under the table, up the stairs.
Dreadful pudding flying around,
Diving quickly to reach the ground.
In an attempt to miss this killer,
Nasty pudding, what a thriller.
Ground is coming closer now, safe at last,

Wow, wow, wow!

Louise Naylor (10)
Richmond House School

THE WEREWOLVES

When the sun goes down,
The werewolves go on the prowl,
They gobble up kids,
And at midnight they howl!

When the sun comes up,
The werewolves go and hide,
Back to their lairs,
Where they wait for the night.

Wilf Mayson (11)
Richmond House School

MY GUINEA PIGS

I have two little guinea pigs
Called Buttercup and Frisky
We keep them inside right now
Because outside it's chilly

I love my guinea pigs very much
I got them from the RSPCA
They live in a little green hutch
And I bathed them yesterday (with some shampoo from Santa).

Buttercup is the elder one
She is ginger with some white
Her little squeaks are very cute
And she never ever bites

Frisky is the younger one
She's small and very sweet
She likes to lick the salt wheel
And runs on her little spotty feet (they're spotty underneath).

Molly Harper (8)
Richmond House School

HOT AND COLD

In summer and spring,
The sun is caring,
It's shining for you and me.
These two are the best,
I'm always impressed,
Never distressed!

In winter and fall,
There's snow and there's rain,
Pouring both day and night.
It pitters and pats
And splitters and splats,
We have to wear hats!

There are seasons four,
Of hot and cold,
Winter, spring, summer and fall.
In summer it glows,
In winter we froze,
That's how it goes!

Lucy Worstenholme (8)
Richmond House School

A SEASON'S POEM

In the winter wrap up warm,
As the strong wind will blow.
All across the land and seas
And cover them with snow.

In the spring chicks start to hatch,
Leaves grow back on all the trees.
Calves grow and begin to walk
And flowers are filled with bees.

In the summer people sunbathe,
As the sun is strong and bright.
All the days are warm and clear
And so are all the nights.

In the autumn leaves turn brown
And yellow and gold and red.
Squirrels start to hibernate
And all the flowers are dead.

Rachel Zagajewski (11)
Richmond House School

WHEN I MET AN OLD TEACHER

When I met an old teacher
she asked me, '2 + 2?'
I said, 'I do not know,
but how about you?'

When I met an old teacher
she kicked me up my bum
I said, 'What's that for?'
She said, 'For beating up my mum.'

When I met an old teacher
She said, 'Let's have some fun.'
So we played kickball
Until she felt young.

When I met an old teacher
For the last time
She said, 'What shall we do?'
I said, 'Let's complete this rhyme.'

Tanis Isaac (9)
Richmond House School

WHY DON'T FISH FLY?

Why don't fish fly
like a bird?
Why don't turtles run
like a hare?
But what does a fishy-wishy do?

Why don't cats swim
like a fish?
Why don't cats catch
like an athlete?
But what does a fishy-wishy do?

Why don't dogs eat buffalo
like lions?
Why don't dogs eat their young
like the dinosaurs?
But what does a fishy-wishy do?

Why don't dragonflies breathe fire
like dragons?
Why don't flies fly planes
like a pilot?
But what does a fishy-wishy do?

Sebastian Erkults (9)
Richmond House School

MY HOBBIES

Rugby, rugby,
Brutal on the games field
But not messy or brutal on the PlayStation.

Hockey, hockey,
Hit the ball really hard,
Whoops! It's hit the fruit stall!

Football, football,
Whack! It's in the goal
The Wakefield Trolls have won.

Tennis, tennis,
Bounce the ball up and down
Then pounce and hit the ball.

Running, running,
Run all the way home, have a shower
And then doze off and finally fall asleep,
                              Zzzzzz!

Georgina Isle
Richmond House School

LIMERICKS

A mole in his burrow
Is in great sorrow.
The reason that -
A great big bat
Attempted to steal instead of borrow.

An old man,
Built a dam,
He made it from mortar -
To keep out the water
But it drowned his mother's ram.

A driving vampire,
Lost a car tyre.
It was made out of rubber -
Mixed in with flubber
But in the end it caught fire.

Barnaby McMahon (10)
Richmond House School

A Dolphin's Hopes And Dreams For The Future

I swim around from place to place,
I'm like a spaceship alone in space,
But down here no space, no fish,
No other dolphins or sharks.
I feel alone, no, I am alone.

Am hoping that it will all change this year,
I'm liked a used-up cloth that no one wants,
Or a ripped-up rug.
I feel alone, no, I am alone.

Everyone's afraid of me, I don't know why,
Fish think I will eat them.
Sharks think I will kill them
But I won't, I'm friendlier than a fish,
Kinder than a shark.
I feel alone, no, I am alone.

Hollie-Elise Kitchen (11)
Rothwell CE I&J School

THE FIELD MOUSE'S FEELINGS

The summer is yellow and bright,
It's warm and inviting,
I jump and skip through the corn,
Enjoying every minute of life.

And then an enormous monster
Comes plodding along, everything turns black,
I am a nervous wreck,
I close my eyes, I know I won't survive.

Then,
    Bang!
        Bang!
            Bang!
                The monster plods off.

I open my eyes,
I wonder what has happened,
There is no corn anywhere,
My home is wrecked and ruined.

I sleep, worrying what will turn out,
I wake up and go outside,
A ray of sunlight shines upon my back
And I am filled with happiness.

Lucy Winterbottom (11)
Rothwell CE I&J School

A Fox's Feelings

I am never safe -
that's why I keep on running.
My pack is terrified
and 'they' think it's funny!
I cannot sleep,
I am too scared . . .
to leave the real world -
unprepared.
I am startled
by the slightest sound,
for they could come -
from all around.
What can I do?
I cannot beat . . .
those terrible 'things' -
with hands and feet.
We only bite for self-defence
shall we run?
I can't decide, I am too tense.
I never thought a world could be
as horrid and nasty -
as this world I dare to see.
Shall I run?
Shall I hide?
Either way I can't decide.
I know!
I'll take my pack somewhere safe.
Or am I being stupid -
there's no such place!

Bethany Spencer (10)
Rothwell CE I&J School

WHY AM I THE BAD ONE?

Why am I the bad one?
The one who is always blamed?
The sneaky prowler
Ready to pounce . . .
On any passers-by
I need to prove
Although you'll doubt
Everything I say
That I am, of course . . .
No more horrible than you!
For you're the ones who scream
And scare *me*
Out of my furry skin!
You, catch me in a cage
And take me to the zoo!
Yet you get the money
They pay
For coming to disturb me.
My friends deep in the jungle
All miss me deep in heart
I'm named 'The King'
For my kindness
Not for acting out the role of bad
In films
In horror movies
In the circus
We animals can't cope with being laughed at
Daily . . .
By public and people like

You!

Megan Elyse Burwell (10)
Rothwell CE I&J School

THE OWL'S WISHES

Sometimes I think no one thinks of me
when it's freezing cold and dark.
I admit I am scared of the shadows,
that wait to pounce on me.

I hunt for my babies but hardly get a thing
for I am to be careful for foxes are around,
and to think I am still alive this day
is a real shock to me.

For those who think I am cruel and wicked,
at least I am not as cruel as the fox
and the stray cats that fight at night.

I only wish that I could survive,
with no cold, no hunters,
no hunger, just peace.
Just listen to me, please listen to me!
Is that too much to ask?

Ruth Cressall (11)
Rothwell CE I&J School

HUMPH!

He's back with his long, sharp, shiny nails
about to scratch my black, soft, lovely, nice coat.
He thinks he strokes me nice and gently
and which I definitely wish for . . .
Oh, if only I had the most wishes in the world
and they would . . .
and they would be . . .
to get out of this old wooden hutch
and be free . . .
like a bird in the fields . . .
and live in a nice cosy burrow
I wouldn't be scratched by Billy's long nails
nearly pulling off my soft quilted coat
although . . .
I might miss eating those milky, soft chocolate buttons.

Dean Nuttall (11)
Rothwell CE I&J School

THE ODD MAN

As I walked along the street
I met a man with two odd feet.
He was wearing funny clothes.
He had a long and pointed nose.
His shoes had split so they showed his toes!
His hair was scraggy, golden too!
His eyes were odd, one black, one blue.
One leg was short, one leg was long.
As he walked he sang a song!
If I see this man again -
I'll be sure to ask his name.

Stephanie Lawson (9)
Rothwell Victoria Junior School

BLAZING THE SUN

Blazing the sun
Slashing claws with a red face,
Tail whipping across the land,
Burning fingers touching the Earth.
Past the sunny house
And hot gardens of roses,
Down from the shimmering blue sky.
Blazing the sun
Scorching, scorching,
Tail whipping, claws slashing,
Burning, burning,
Down over the streets and the dry fields.
Blazing the sun
A fiery beast scorching the land.

Stacey Jefferson (9)
Rothwell Victoria Junior School

BRIGHTLY THE LIGHTNING

Brightly the lightning,
Fork-tongued with a dark fuse.
Claws sharp destroy,
Tail crashing the way,
Past the dark gardens of graves.
Down from the grey clouds,
Brightly the lightning,
Flashing, flashing,
Claws sharp, fork-tongued,
Hunting, hunting,
Across the sky to the roof tops.

Brightly the lightning.

Rebecca Parker (9)
Rothwell Victoria Junior School

BLAZING THE SUN

Blazing the sun,
Bursting fire with a red face,
Hot teeth, scorching,
Burning mouth, breathing flames,
Hot fire on the land,
Baking the ground.
From the hot fiery skies,
Blazing the sun,
Flaming, flaming,
Red face, bursting fire,
Boiling, boiling.
Flames licking round the floor,
Blazing the sun,
A hot fire-breathing dragon burning the Earth.

Connor Anthony Scott (9)
Rothwell Victoria Junior School

SPARKLING THE SUN

Sparkling the sun
Bright beams with a sparkling face,
Glittering in the sky, sinking,
Some glances of light touching the way,
Past the warm houses
And gleaming fountains.
Sparkling the sun
Sinking, sinking,
Glittering in the sky, bright beams,
Leaving, leaving,
Down beneath the trees,
Sparkling the sun,
The yellow jewel settling down on the land.

Jessica Ley (9)
Rothwell Victoria Junior School

SOMEWHERE IN OUR SCHOOL TODAY

Somewhere in our school today,
Somewhere in our school today,
Children work quietly revising for SATs,
Year 3 and 4 play noisily.
Somewhere in our school today,
Teachers shout frustratingly,
Children playing football quickly.
Somewhere in our school today,
Children waiting hopefully for the home time bell restlessly.
Somewhere in our school today,
Dinner ladies serving patiently,
Children being handed out homework disastrously.
Somewhere in our school today,
Children getting ready for PE quietly,
A child's parent comes round shyly.
Somewhere in our school today,
Children listening to their teacher explaining,
Children getting restless.

Ashlea Cunningham (10)
Rothwell Victoria Junior School

Softly the Snow

Softly the snow,
Wings spread with a white face,
Feathers fluttering, floating,
Wing tips touching the way,
Onto the bare branches,
And flying around and around
For some food.
Softly the snow,
Flying, flying,
Feathers fluttering, wings spread,
Floating, floating,
Slowly flying down to the ground.
Softly the snow,
A feather floating lightly down.

Rebecca Kellegher (10)
Rothwell Victoria Junior School

Play Time

P   eople shouting and calling to their friends
L   aughter from the children who tell each other jokes.
A   pples lying half-eaten in the bins.
Y   ou can just see magpies and blackbirds pecking worms
                                          at the top of the field.

T   eachers reassuring children about their grazed knees.
I   ce cream van parked at the gates while the children's mouths water.
M   arigolds dancing around in their pots caused by the wind.
E   veryone happily playing together.

Kirstie Backhouse (11)
Rothwell Victoria Junior School

CATS

Furry and cute,
fat and skinny,
wild ones and pet ones,
black and white,
ginger or grey,
large, small or kitten.
Persian or Siamese,
tabby or tortoiseshell.
Every one of these loves
sleeping and eating,
nothing else can beat it.
On their lonesome
or with their owner.
Each cat likes to be a loner.
Affection and love
is all of the above.
A simple miaow means a
million times now . . .
I want a hug,
I want a drink,
I want food
and most of all I want
you!

Ellen Watson (10)
Rothwell Victoria Junior School

THE PINK UNDERWEAR

Nobody lives in the fort anymore,
It was abandoned right after the war.
Nobody knows how long it has stood,
All alone in the fields of mud.
My friend dared me to go right in,
He said if I didn't he would poke me with a pin.
So I silently crept through the door
And stood around, gazing in awe,
As suddenly appearing on the stair,
A soldier's ghost in pink underwear!
I screamed and screamed and my friend came in,
'Go touch Ghosty Pants unless you're chicken!'
As I started climbing the stair,
The ghost disappeared with the pink underwear.
We stood screaming then ran out of the house,
Followed closely by 2,000 woodlice.
We saw a boy who said, 'You're screaming, please stop it.'
We said, 'We know, so you hop it.'
The mystery of the pink underwear,
We wish it would just get out of our hair.

Gemma Wilson (11)
Rothwell Victoria Junior School

SOMEWHERE IN OUR SCHOOL TODAY

Somewhere in our school today
The anxious head teacher plucks out another grey hair secretly
Class 5DW work silently, creatively, scribbling down a poem.
Somewhere in our school today
The dinnertime bell rings
Children are greedily drooling for their dinner
Children shouting loudly, wanting to get into the
                              swimming pool excitedly.
Somewhere in our school today
Children are reading silently
Year 4 shouting loudly while doing PE
Somewhere in our school today
Years 5 and 6 are silently working
Years 3 and 4 are running around the playground.

Somewhere in our school today
Teachers and helpers are running to the photocopier
                              to photocopy worksheets
Class 5DW are reading some letters about fox-hunting.
Somewhere in our school today
The dinner time staff are setting the tables and cooking
                              dinner for the children
The head teacher is talking to the secretary.
Somewhere in our school today . . .

Claire Comer (10)
Rothwell Victoria Junior School

MILLY, MY PUPPY-DOG

I wish I had a puppy-dog
I'd like to call her Milly
I know I'd love her very much
And she would love me too.
We'd take a ball into the park
And run and play around
Then home we'd go for our tea
Tired and worn out.

Then one day my wish came true
I could not believe my eyes
For there in front of me
Sat one little homeless pup
Who, when she saw me, wagged her tail
That was the sign for me
This was Milly for sure
So home with me she'd be!

Jessica Murrell (9)
Rothwell Victoria Junior School

FRIGHT IN THE NIGHT

When I was walking up to bed
I heard a noise from up ahead
so I went to the loft and what did I see?
I saw an enormously big creature.

It sat on a log staring
so I tried to sneak to it
but it heard me and turned around
and began to growl and stare at me.

It had a pair of big googly eyes
and it was really hairy
it tried to grab me but I ran
so it ran after me.

I began to scream
but I knew my mum would hear me
so I decided to shut up instead
my mum heard me so I tried to shut the loft up.

My mum came up and went to bed
so I opened it up again
the monster had gone
suddenly I felt a claw on my back!

Then I woke up
it was all a dream
so I went downstairs and heard
a noise from up ahead!

Aiden Packer (9)
Rothwell Victoria Junior School

CHILDREN

Children can be oh so sweet
even though they smell of feet.
They hide under tables and chairs
and snuggle up to their toys and bears.
They give you a cuddle with a smile
and jump on you to form a pile.
Children can be oh so sweet
and sit with you on a seat.
Children under the age of five
are really active and alive.
Even though they fall a lot
they might act like a *robot!*
If you see them in the bins
they'll end up looking like ugly things.
Children can be oh so sweet
even though they smell like feet.

Nina Harbour (11)
Rothwell Victoria Junior School

ICE CREAM

I like ice cream a whole lot.
It tastes good when days are hot.
In a cone or in a dish, this could be my only wish.
Ding, dang, dong, can you hear the ice cream man's song?
The children like to hear the rhyme.
Hooray, hooray, ice cream time!
Chocolate, strawberry, vanilla too.
100 flavours just for you.
Lollipops, ice pops, cans of pop too.
Lots of cold things waiting for you.
Mind that child, the van says.
Beware of children coming your way.
Slow down, keep them safe and well.
Remember when you hear the bell.
Ice cream is for happy times.
Thank goodness I've finished this silly rhyme!

Laura Portrey (11)
Rothwell Victoria Junior School

THE THINGAMABOB

The thingamabob
Loves his job
In the middle of the night
The thingamabob
Loves his job
It gives me quite a fright
The thingamabob
Loves his job
In the night-time school
The thingamabob
Loves his job
Playing a game of pool
The thingamabob
Loves his job
Being in the council
The thingamabob
Loves his job
Bouncing up and down still
The thingamabob
Loves his job
Being all alone
The thingamabob
Loves his job
Talking on the phone
The thingamabob
Loves his job
Flying in the air
The thingamabob
Loves his job
Eating a little pear.

Rosie Zanetti (10)
Rothwell Victoria Junior School

HEAVILY THE RAIN

Heavily the rain,
Cold and wet with a dripping face,
Screeching claws, advances,
Sharp nails feeling the way,
Lurking over the dark houses
And the dead rose gardens,
Down the steep muddy hill.
Heavily the rain,
Dropping, dropping,
Cold and wet, dripping face,
Searching, searching
Out through and into the city,
Heavily the rain,
Needles slashing down to Earth.

Rachel Kennedy (11)
Rothwell Victoria Junior School

MY HEART

My heart is full with happiness
My heart is full with joy
But if doesn't get better if you're a boy!
My heart is full with wishes and surprise
But it doesn't get better if you're a boy!
My heart is full with danger
My heart is full with mysteries
But it doesn't get better if you're a boy!

Hennah Kiran (9)
Royal Park Primary School

WINTER - CINQUAIN

Winter
Snowy mornings
It is too cold to sleep
It is too cold for anything
So cold.

Sanya Ikram (9)
Royal Park Primary School

JANUARY NIGHT - CINQUAIN

Waking
deadly cold and . . .
shiver, icicles fall,
dark night, snow drifts, black night, owls hoot
Listen . . .

Megan Parker (9)
Royal Park Primary School

BONFIRE NIGHT - CINQUAIN

See that
Like flames above
A dragon's fiery breath
Crackling . . . fiery dots of colour
Darkness.

Coran Sloss (10)
Royal Park Primary School

I WAKE - CINQUAIN

I wake
Don't remember
Cold rushes over me
Out the window snow is falling
So cold.

Carlo Corey (10)
Royal Park Primary School

HOT SUMMER - CINQUAIN

Summer . . .
Is here, sun's out
Shining bright, sun's too hot
Holidays, sea, sand, back again
Hot sun.

Haleema Iqbal (11)
Royal Park Primary School

SPRING NIGHT - CINQUAIN

Spring night
The frozen cars
Door stuck, now what to do?
Water frozen, birds can't drink it
New shoots.

Kes Mansoor (11)
Royal Park Primary School

SNOWBALL - CINQUAIN

Slap, bang . . .
It is coming
Zooming fast towards you
White ball made out of snow hits you
Lie there . . .

Adnan Ghafoor (9)
Royal Park Primary School

TIGER

T   he fast sniper,
I   ts pounce, how great!
G   ets its prey,
E   very time,
R   ips its prey to pieces,
    I want to be a . . . !

Libby Crane (8)
Royal Park Primary School

WINTER - CINQUAIN

Winter
It is too cold
It will be raining snow
I will be able to see snow
Listen.

Donald Chitembwe (10)
Royal Park Primary School

A FAST STRIKER

A fast striker
a mountain hiker
a six-week shredder
a baby bedder
a mouse ripper
a tree chipper
a fast climber
a heat sensor
it gets tension
a lip licker
a tongue flicker
a venom spurter
a human hurter
a catalogue to make me a snake!

Cameron Robinson (9)
Royal Park Primary School

A SUPER STINGER

A super stinger,
A neck ringer,
A light maker,
An octopus copier,
A tentacle bearer
A known killer
A catalogue to make me . . .
A jellyfish.

Owen Corey (9)
Royal Park Primary School

I WILL PUT IN THE BOX
(Based on 'Magic Box' by Kit Wright)

I will put in the box . . .
a red ruby star.
I will put in the box . . .
a sparkly diamond.
I will put in the box . . .
a big shiny rocket.
I will put in the box . . .
a fresh dhal butty.
I will put in the box . . .
poisonous monkey blood.
I will put in the box . . .
a glowing love heart.
I will put in the box . . .
a twinkle from my mother's eye.
I will put in the box . . .
a big earring.
I will put in the box . . .
a million-pound cheque.
I will put in the box . . .
a shiny golden flower.
I will put in the box . . .
a gold octopus leg.
I will put in the box . . .
A moonlight crystal
I will put in the box . . .
orange soda.
I will put in the box . . .
a silver toy brain.
I will put in the box . . .
two-headed pencils with four goggly eyes.

I will put in the box . . .
a shiny golden ring.
I will put in the box . . .
a photo of my family.

Ayesha Shafiq Rehman (9)
Royal Park Primary School

LEEDS UNITED!

Kewell to Mills
Mills to Smith
Watch out, I smell a whiff!
Smith has scored
Man U are going down
And their fans start to frown
Beckham shoots it in the net
Oh no, it's now one-all!
Leeds' fans roar
The rain begins to pour.

Milner to Barmby
Barmby to Milner
Will they ever score this year?
Terry's getting worried
We're getting buried
Kewell shoots it in the net
That's good because
Everyone's getting wet
Only two minutes left of the game
I think Leeds will have some fame
Man U are in big shame!

Thomas Eyles (10)
St Matthew's CE Primary School

THE MOON

The moon is a sparkling light bulb
in the cold, dark house.
A moon is a shimmering snowflake
coming from the sky.
Our moon is a scoop of ice cream
in a white bowl.
It's round and calm and cools people down
and is fun to watch at night.

Tiffany Lawrence (10)
St Matthew's CE Primary School

DISEASE

Disease is mouldy green,
It smells like methane,
Disease tastes sickly and disgusting,
It sounds like the screaming of the dead,
It looks ugly and horrible,
Disease lives in a pit of bubbling tar.

Jack Hallas (9)
St Matthew's CE Primary School

THE MOON

The moon is a dazzling light bulb,
A moon is a mirror of light,
Our moon is a rolling snowball,
It dazzles through the night,
The moon is a dazzling light bulb,
Shining through the night.

Scott Haining (10)
St Matthew's CE Primary School

THE MOON

This moon is a round silver ball.
The moon is a peeled potato.
Our moon is a light bulb.

The moon is a scoop of ice cream.
Our moon is a white painted mirror.
This moon is a silver eye.

Monica Rooprai (10)
St Matthew's CE Primary School

WAR

War is *blood-red,*
It smells like burning petrol
And tastes like sprouts,
War sounds like screaming babies,
It looks hideous
And it lives in the glint of an evil man's eye.

Ben Jenkins (10)
St Matthew's CE Primary School

THE MOON

The moon is a cold snowball, shimmering at night.
My shiny ice ball is looking after me all night
This moon is a mirror shining on the river.
My shimmering moon is lighting the way for us all.

Amy Sylvester (10)
St Matthew's CE Primary School

THE MOON

The moon is like a disco ball
it's a shimmering ball of steel.
The moon is a smiling staring face
it's a glistening pearl in the sky.
It's a giant silver circle
and a shiny see-through snowball.

I love the moon.

Tom McFadyen (10)
St Matthew's CE Primary School

DEATH

Death is the smell of rotting bodies.
Death is the taste of a disease.
Death is very painful.
Death is the sound of screaming.
Death is the colour of *killer red.*

Death is still out there!

Ajay Kumar (10)
St Matthew's CE Primary School

THE WIND, MOON AND THE ROAD

The wind was a draught of a hairdryer,
The moon was a ball of boiling fire,
The road was a crooked man's back
And the headless ghost came gliding, gliding, gliding!
The headless ghost came gliding up to the spooky palace.

Suraiya Bertie (10)
St Matthew's CE Primary School

WIND

The wind is a grizzly bear
Come out to play if you dare!
The wind is like a howling hound
Be careful it might lift you off the ground!

But beware of the vicious tornado
We all know he's a terrible foe;
He'll flatten your two-storey home
And steal away your garden gnome!

The wind isn't always that bad,
Sometimes it can make you feel glad.
When you're flying a kite,
Just look at that amazing sight.

Rosemary Pollock (10)
St Matthew's CE Primary School

CATS AND DOGS

Cats are always purring,
Annoying it may be,
The cats don't do it on purpose,
They're as happy as can be.
Sleeping all day long
And hunting through the night,
Never like dogs.
Dogs are always guarding,
Dogs are always running,
On the street they greet their friends,
Give them a bone, they chomp and gnaw,
So cute their bark is, nothing like cats!

Natalie Atherton (9)
St Matthew's CE Primary School

WALKING LONELY AS A SPIDER

A spider in a house
Goes unnoticed
Like a mouse,
For no butterflies live.

A spider in the gutter
Crawls amongst the clutter,
For no butterflies live.

A spider on the gravel
Finds it cannot travel.
Its eight crooked legs
Are like wooden pegs
The butterfly soars
The gravel it ignores.

In the plants
The spiders dance
And the butterflies live.

Harry Crocker (9)
St Matthew's CE Primary School

DEATH

Death is blood-red
It smells like rotten eggs
Death tastes like rotten fish
It sounds like screaming
It looks like a shadow
Death lives down the drain.

Josie Moulton (9)
St Matthew's CE Primary School

I AM THE TIGER

Pouncing, pouncing gently it goes
until one glimmer of its prey

I am the tiger.

Running masses of metres for its prey,
it leaps viciously onto it

I am the tiger.

Suffocating its prey, it tears away
the fleshy carcass to feed its family.

I am the tiger.

Hunted down, hunted down,
like foxes we will soon be extinct.

I am the tiger!

Callum Armstrong (11)
St Matthew's CE Primary School

DOLPHINS

Dolphins splashing in the cool water,
The hot sun beaming down on them,
Dolphins are jumping through hoops,
They are playing with balls and bouncing them on their noses,
Making squealing noises as they play,
Jumping high above the water
And having races too
As they argue who won and who lost,
They dive deep into the light blue water.

Anna Simpson (11)
St Matthew's CE Primary School

SPAGHETTI!

Spaghetti, spaghetti
Slurpy and wriggly
Grandma's spaghetti sauce is spicy.

Spaghetti, spaghetti,
Hot spices, peppers and chilli
Long, thin spaghetti.

Spaghetti, spaghetti
Grandad's spaghetti is jumpy
You can get spaghetti Bolognese, yummy.

Spaghetti, spaghetti
Mint sauce with spaghetti
Blueberry liquid on top of spaghetti, munchy!

Spaghetti, spaghetti
Eat it, eat it, saucy and fine is spaghetti
And you are mine because you're divine
Spaghetti, long, thin spaghetti!

Aine O'Donnell (11)
St Matthew's CE Primary School

RAINFOREST TREE

I sway all day in the warm summer day.
I throw monkeys from tree to tree,
I can hear them but they can't hear me.
I feel the ants tickle my roots
And birds on my branches whistle and toot.
When it's windy, I hold myself strong
And when it's cold I whistle my song.
Hot, moist and free, I love my life as a rainforest tree.

Pascale Metcalf (11)
St Matthew's CE Primary School

LITTLE BABIES

What's with all the grown-ups?
They keep ignoring me
and making a fuss of that pile of fluff
that's lying next to me.
What's the big attraction?
All it does is eat and poop.
Maybe it's an alien cos it keeps going 'Ga-ga-gu.'
Later on I found out it was not an alien
it was my baby brother wanting to join in the fun.

Nicole Noble (11)
St Matthew's CE Primary School

PEACE

Peace is a creamy white colour
With a sweet strawberry bonbon taste to it,
Her smell is of freshly cut flowers from a field,
She sounds like the sea moving softly, at the seaside
And she feels like cotton wool,
She lives in the countryside.

Ruth Trick (9)
St Matthew's CE Primary School

POWER

Power is like gold and silver
It tastes as good as chocolate ice cream
Power is as pleasant as flowers
It sounds like horns and fireworks
It feels fantastic!

Daniel Blissett (10)
St Matthew's CE Primary School

THE BIG GIANT MAGNET

This was the day
Far, far away
A big magnet in the air
Picking up cars and smashing them down
People screaming all around
Getting themselves into the house
Praying it could turn into a mouse.
Bigger than humans it floated around
Picking up cars and smashing them down.

It was an alarming day
Far, far away
For those people in town
But they managed to shoot the *giant magnet* down!

Laura Wood (11)
St Matthew's CE Primary School

VOLCANO

I spit like a snake and bubble in rage and anger.
When I am angry I erupt and spit out hot lava.
I can be found in most places and I can be any size.
If anyone gets in my way they burn to ashes
Because of my boiling, bubbling lava.
I melt down houses and burn down trees.
I can also be calm but I'm still very deadly.

What am I?

Ashley Skillington (11)
St Matthew's CE Primary School

A CHAMELEON

Poor little chameleon
walking step by step,
down on the sandy road,
roasting, I bet.
In the distant dusk, I see a little cloud
then I shout out loud
'Something's coming, what can it be?
Let's take a closer look and see!
Oh no!'
In that little dusty cloud,
something comes closer,
a lorry man,
in his van,
better move,
splat!
'Bye-bye,
you poor little chameleon.'

Grace-Ellen Burch (10)
St Matthew's CE Primary School

THE EAGLE

When the eagle calls everyone listens.
When the eagle hunts, he hunts you to the ground.
You will be found, found.
He sits so high that he touches the sky so high, so high.
Looks so proud all alone ruling the sky, sky,
Waiting to pounce on his prey, prey.
I am the hunter.
I am strong.
   I am the eagle!

Helene Payiatis (10)
St Matthew's CE Primary School

JEALOUSY REARS ITS UGLY HEAD

All the kids I know
Are so cool
They're talented and gifted
Brainy and cruel

Jamie's got talent
Jody's got looks
Lisa likes Chinese food
But she's an awful cook

Justin's downright naughty
Britney's kindness will pass
Whenever she gets chocolate bars
She shares them round our class

Sam is really brainy
He knows everything, you name it!
He knows so much about space
He might as well live on a planet

Kelly's a prima donna
She thinks she's really flash
She wears the latest fashions
And throws away her cash

I don't have talent
I don't have looks
I hate Chinese food
And I don't know how to cook

Whenever I think of my friends in my head
Jealousy rears its ugly head!

Helen Ukoh (10)
St Matthew's CE Primary School

MY BABY COUSIN

My baby cousin
is so snotty,
she is a girl
and she normally does potty.

It is so nasty,
that it reeks
and her wee
normally leaks.

It trickles down her legs,
like syrup on a spoon,
it tickles her a lot
and she loves prunes.

She eats them with jam,
or sometimes with toast,
but best of all,
with roast.

She likes them on a plate,
sometimes on the floor,
even worse on the toilet,
and her attitude is very poor.

She acts like a cat
and crawls all over the floor,
she eats like a pig,
roar!
I'm done with her,
I've had enough,
it wasn't that bad,
but sometimes she thinks she's rough.

What can I do?
It's just life!

Natasha Nasir (11)
St Matthew's CE Primary School

THE WHITE KITTEN

The tiny kitten looks like a cotton wool ball,
The kitten has soft white fur,
She is playing in the soft white snow,
She looks like a fluffy cloud,
Then she goes inside,
The kitten plays with wool,
The pure white kitten is playing
And purring as the day goes by,
She sleeps soundlessly at night,
She then wakes up,
She gets bored and explores upstairs.

Harriet Simpson (11)
St Matthew's CE Primary School

CROCODILE

I can make you petrified with one look at my face
And my tail is long and smooth in every place.

I can rip you up and tear your skin,
Or you could try to fight. Why bother? You know I'd win!

Bodies I can rip and insides I can eat.
I can go on land or in water; whichever, I can slaughter.

When I am cross I can tear and kill
And when I am happy I was made to thrill!

Bethany Wilson (10)
St Matthew's CE Primary School

CHICKENS

Chickens, chickens
Look out below
Chickens, chickens
Get with the flow

Chickens, chickens
They can't fly
Chickens, chickens
And that you can't deny

Chickens, chickens
They live on a farm
Chickens, chickens
Inside a barn

Chickens, chickens
When they feed
Chickens, chickens
They eat a lot of seed

Chickens, chickens
They taste really nice
Chickens, chickens
Especially with rice

Chickens, chickens
Look out below
Chickens, chickens
Get with the flow.

James Tatt (10)
St Matthew's CE Primary School

PERSONIFICATION POEM

I can see through the seas with big beady eyes
and I leap out of water doing flips and dives.
I can sometimes swim in a group, moving round and round
or I glide through the water not touching the ground.
I have a beak like a snout with which I can catch fish like trout.
When I am underwater I feel smooth and silky to the touch
and most creatures like me, but the killer whale? Not much!

Emma Croft (11)
St Matthew's CE Primary School

DEATH

Death is coal-black,
With a taste of burnt toast,
He smells of thick grey smoke,
When passing he deafens
With the scream of a witch,
He feels like the ice-cold North Pole wind,
And lives in the fires of Hell!

Sarah Griffin (10)
St Matthew's CE Primary School

LOVE

Love is pale red,
With a taste like a banana.
Love smells like roses,
Sounds like a sweet, sweet flute.
Love feels like soft baby oil,
It lives in the heavenly sky.

Georgina Skillington (9)
St Matthew's CE Primary School

PEACE

Peace is heavenly blue
She tastes of cool Cornetto
Smells of creme bath bubbles
The sweet sound of birds singing in the dawn
She feels like a big fluffy cloud
And lives in sunny blue Heaven.

Tramaine Higgins
St Matthew's CE Primary School

DEATH

Death's colour is black.
He tastes like blood.
He smells like a lamb to the slaughter.
Death sounds like a screeching rat.
He feels painful like a deep cut.
He can live wherever there's life.

Jamil Jeffreys (9)
St Matthew's CE Primary School

DEATH

Death is cold, slate-grey,
She tastes burnt and bitter.
She smells like sooty smoke.
Death scrapes like nails on a blackboard,
She's cold like frozen water
And lives in the fires of Hell.

Jake Shipley (10)
St Matthew's CE Primary School

POWER

Power's colour is dark gold
He tastes as sweet as sweet chocolate
And smells as strong as spicy curry
Power sounds like a trumpet playing the National Anthem
And he is strong and hard
And Power lives in a mansion for he is a knight.

Joseph Martinicca (9)
St Matthew's CE Primary School

I LIKE HAM

What I hate about ham is
The way it is from a pig
It's awful!

What I like about ham is
The way it is pink.

What I hate about ham is
All the different ways they make it
Because it comes in all shapes and sizes.

What I like about ham is
The way it tastes yummy
When I swallow it.

What I hate about ham is
The way it can make you fat
So you go big.

Amy Clarkson (7)
Sharp Lane Primary School

CANDY AND ME

Candy and me are the best of friends
but sometimes she drives me around the bend
I give her some hay for her to eat
and when she eats it she looks so sweet
I put her saddle upon her back
then we'll go for a hack
Over hills, across the meadows
blowing trees and honeybees
They sky is growing dark
clouds settle above the park
So me and Candy set off home
then I'll give her a soothing comb.

Rebecca Cawood (11)
Sharp Lane Primary School

I HATE SWEETCORN

What I hate about sweetcorn is it is too sweet
so I have to have a drink straight after.

What I like about sweetcorn is the colour
because it is as light as the stars.

What I hate about sweetcorn is when you eat it altogether
you can feel it so crumbly.

What I like about sweetcorn is the little hard bits
which you pick out with your fork.

Colleen Mooney (8)
Sharp Lane Primary School

QUAD BIKING

Getting ready
Off I go
Gloves on
Out to the snow
Down the road
Helmet on tight
All powered up
I take flight
Wind in my eyes
It takes me by surprise
I lose control
I slip and slide
I fall to the ground on my backside
It could have been worse
I could have died!

Sam Parker (10)
Sharp Lane Primary School

I LIKE LIONS

What I hate about lions is
they attack and eat animals.

What I like about lions is
their jungle-yellow fur.

What I hate about lions is
their large white fangs which hang out of their mouth.

What I like about lions is
their beautiful, long, orange mane.

Launa Senior (7)
Sharp Lane Primary School

MY OLD GRANDAD

My old grandad sits in his armchair
Going on about being in the war, although he wasn't there
He says he was the only survivor
He was only 13, says my nan, Eliza.

His favourite saying is, 'In my day
We had none of these game consoles, neh, neh, neh.'
My dad says he's raving mad
Grandad still treats dad like a lad.

He lives with us but mum says, 'Put him in a home
Then we wouldn't have to listen to him moan.'
He sits in his room reading books
Looking at his allegedly good looks.

I asked for the strongest animal, he said a mouse
He then corrected himself with a woodlouse
The thing that really flipped Mum's lid
Was when he brought home his own pet squid.

So Mum put him in a home called Mave
He argued a lot, but I think he's lucky not to be in a grave
Although we moan, Grandad hath
The ability to make the whole family laugh.

Christopher Day (10)
Sharp Lane Primary School

MY LITTLE BROTHER

My little brother is full of lies,
When he's hungry he fills his face full of pies.
His favourite pleasure is breaking my toys,
I'm sick and tired of naughty little boys.

My brother thinks he's fantastic,
His brain must be made of plastic.
He runs madly around the house,
Thinking he's brave but I think he's a mouse.

My brother broke a plate
And blamed it on my best mate.
When he grows up he wants to be a scientist in inflation,
But I think he's going to end up in a police station.

Beau Procter (11)
Sharp Lane Primary School

EARLY IN THE MORNING

I wake up in the morning
I lay back, I'm still yawning
My mum she shouts out loud
It's time to get up now
I try to stretch my arm up high
But I cannot lift one muscle
I hear her shout out loud again
Come on, get up!
Please get up now!
You need to go to school
I just will have a few more minutes
In my comfy bed.

Abbie Elliott (11)
Sharp Lane Primary School

ARCHERY

I take my bow and arrow
And aim for the board
I pull back my hand
I have a careful eye
On the bullseye.

I let go of the arrow
Whoosh, see it go
Cutting through the air
With no care.

Like a blade
It never fades
'Bullseye!' I cry
I have scored
Oh thank you Lord.

Simon Atkinson (10)
Sharp Lane Primary School

FANTASY WORLD

The sunset was forming as I pounded over the hill
I took a big leap and peeped over the mill
I pushed through the undergrowth and made my way to the castle
Next to the castle there was a tree
Whose leaves look like tassels
I saw a rainbow, a bird and a dream
As I walked towards the sea
I felt something swallow me
Inside there was a boat with a sail
I realised I'd been swallowed by a . . .
Whale!

Jade Brierley (11)
Sharp Lane Primary School

COMPUTASTIC!

Sitting in front of the screen,
Sometimes I can scream,
I'm typing up a document,
When the computer freezes.

I'm finding out what's wrong with it,
I think it needs to go get fit,
Adding more memory is a good idea,
Maybe even a DVD player.

A hard disc making it fast,
Slow is a word of the past,
Internet whizzing by,
Technology in your eye.

This programme is fun,
I'll make it number one,
Take the old programme out,
Put the new one in.

Computastic is fantastic!

Jonathan Watt (11)
Sharp Lane Primary School

ME, MY FRIEND AND PENNY

Me, my friend and penny,
We go to sleep at night,
Penny ends up waking up,
And giving us a fright.

We wake up in the morning,
Then we start to shout,
Penny starts crying,
We say we're going out.

Where are you going?
When are you coming back?
Don't be long,
Where is my mac?

When we get back
We run up the stairs,
I turn my music on
And get out my flares.

We've got a party to go to,
Must get our make-up on,
When Penny comes looking,
We'll be long gone.

Danielle Sugden (11)
Sharp Lane Primary School

THE BIKE RACE

We put our helmets on
Zooming down the hill
Getting faster and faster
Look at me go!
Number sixteen, I'm in the lead
Number twenty catching up
He takes over number sixteen
Oh! He's fallen off his bike
Sixteen, I'm back in the lead
Zooming past him now
We're drawing
We're nearly at the finish line
Can I win?
Yes of course I can
I'm near the finish line
I won, I won!
The crowd go wild.

Kyle Holmes 10)
Sharp Lane Primary School

THE SUN

The sun is
Hot as a hot water bottle snuggled up in bed
Round as a ball kicked into the sky
Orange as a juicy orange just been peeled
Shiny as the moon on a dark, dark night
Makes you relaxed like a dog in the warmth.

Sophie Cass (8)
Sharp Lane Primary School

TOMB SEEKERS, SEEK SECRETS

There was a little secret that went around my room
I felt like I was captured
In a mummy's tomb
This secret went around my head
I felt like I was stuck in bed
The tomb was full of spiderwebs that covered my mind
There was a mummy, he wasn't very kind
A brain in a jar
The colour of it was like a chocolate bar
That secret that was in my room
Now it belongs to this horrid tomb
The mummy kept my secret and locked it in a safe
And away it was blown
And my daring secret was never known.

Natalie Gelderd (10)
Sharp Lane Primary School

WHAT I HATE

I like bananas because they have a sweet taste
I hate to see bananas go to waste
I like the shape of tasty bananas
I eat them in my pyjamas
I hate them warm in the sun so I ask my mum for another one
I like bananas because they are yum, yum
I hate bananas because they fill my tum
I like bananas and monkeys do too
I hate bananas when monkeys go 'Boo!'
I like bananas when they go all spotty
And my mum goes totally potty.

Bethany Tench (8)
Sharp Lane Primary School

GRANDMAS AND GRANDADS

Grandmas are great, Grandad's a star,
If you need them they're near, never far.
They run the bath just for you,
Just in case you smell, *phew!*

The food and cakes that they share
Makes me burst out of the clothes I wear.
They spoil you rotten and give you treats,
I like it best when they give me sweets.

They comfort and cuddle me when I'm feeling down,
Especially when I've got an upset frown.

If you had grandparents just like me,
You'd see how kind they can be!

Casey Brown
Sharp Lane Primary School

WHEN I AM NAUGHTY

When I am naughty
I am a deflated balloon
I am a picture with no colour
I am a radio with no tune
When I am naughty
I am a sandwich with no filling
I am a movie with no picture
I am a TV with no sound
I am not going to be naughty anymore.

Alex Irvin (10)
South Milford School

WHEN I'M NAUGHTY

When I'm naughty I am as useless as . . .
A broken toy
A pen with no ink
A window with no glass.

When I am naughty I am as useless as . . .
A burst balloon
A dictionary of numbers
A house with no roof.

When I am naughty I am as useless as . . .
A pencil with no lead
A clock with no hands
An atlas full of numbers.

Betsy Mallett (10)
South Milford School

WHEN I'M NAUGHTY

When I'm naughty
I am as useless
As a felt tip without a lid
As a butterfly without its wings
As a window with no glass
I am as useless
As a poster with nothing on it
As a TV with no screen
As a dictionary with no words.

Robyn Tanner (10)
South Milford School

HALL HEOROT - IF THE WALLS COULD TALK

They would be proud and stand tall and erect with might
They would rejoice at the new life they had been given
They would admire the beauty that had been bestowed upon them
They would quake on their foundations as Grendel smote upon the door
They would screech with terror as his hideous bulk
Ripped the souls from those around him
They would moan as Grendel extinguished
The flames of life under them
They would whisper their hatred and dream about revenge.

Matthew McHale (11)
South Milford School

WHEN I'M NAUGHTY

When I'm naughty
I am the old book which no one reads
The rusty hook which no one needs
The empty can which is on the floor
The broken pan which got broken on the door.

When I'm naughty
I am the table with only three legs
The ripped up basket with only two pegs
The rusty bottle opener which you can't use
The torn up bouncy ball which you always lose
So I'm going to be good
Like you should.

Jodie Barker (10)
South Milford School

If The Walls Could Talk - Hall Heorot

If the walls could talk they would:
    Love and praise Hrothgar for building Heorot
    Celebrate the great feast with the nine lords
    Shine with pride whenever the poets came to look
    at the magnificent hall.

If the walls would talk they would:
    Cower under the wrath of Grendel
    They would shiver with the cold blood of the nine lords
    splattered on the wall
    And cry out for Hrothgar.

Dominic Hinchley (10)
South Milford School

Kenning - Faye

Good-worker
Raisin-seller
Page-turner
Hair-flicker
Pencil-fiddler
Food-scraper
Chair-swinger
TV-watcher
Brother-tormentor
Food-eater
Cat-carer
Sweet-scoffer
Weekend-clubber.

Faye Glasby (10)
South Milford School

BMX Dudes

The first thing we do
When we get out of school
Is get on our bike
And act really cool

We're so hard
We're so tough
We don't need helmets
Cos we're so good

We do a bunny hop
And a three-sixty turn
We skid so far
Our tyres burn

We're so hard
We're so tough
We don't need helmets
Cos we're so good

Car comes speeding down the street
It knocks Alex off his feet
Alex is in hospital, we visit him
And so does his mate called Tim.

Patrick Dean (10)
South Milford School

WHEN WE GO ON A LONG TRIP

When we go on a long trip in the car
Maybe to a restaurant or bar
I get bored, I want to go to sleep
But all I can hear is *peep, peep, peep!*
I want to read my book, even though it makes me feel sick
So I undo my seat belt, that should do the trick
I happily read my story completely unaware
That the car coming the other way was giving Mum a scare
She swerved and skidded and I banged my head
And when I woke up I thought I was dead
Now when I go on a long trip in the car
Maybe to a restaurant or bar
I wear my seat belt and I keep still
Now I think back and think that cars and speed
Can kill!

Miles Featherstone (10)
South Milford School

A PUDDLE OF FIRE

A building of men
A fact file of nothing
A cookie of sourness
A football pitch of wood
A cemetery of happiness
A pancake of bitterness

A boulder of egg
A whirlwind of flowers
A fireplace of snow
A river of steam
A raindrop of electricity
A puddle of fire.

Owen Wake (11)
South Milford School

I'M WALKING HOME

I'm walking down the busy road,
My reflectors banging my leg,
It's really getting rather dark,
I'm going home to bed.

I've been out in the park,
Playing footie with my mates,
But now it's dark and we're off home,
But I see the bully approach.

I'm scared cos I don't wanna get hurt,
I dash into the road,
A squeal of brakes, a flash of light
A searing pain, I fall.

I hear my mom and dad,
Crying salty tears,
I hear sirens coming,
It all goes quiet and black . . .

Lauren Howley (11)
South Milford School

KENNING - JOSH

PlayStation player
Chair swinger
Pencil chewer
TV watcher
Food gobbler
Pen flicker
SATs dreader
Water drinker.

Joshua Phillips (10)
South Milford School

WHEN I AM NOT CONCENTRATING

When I am not concentrating I am as useless as . . .
A broken fan
An empty cola can.

I am as useless as . . .
A shoe with no heel
A bike with no wheel.

I am as useless as . . .
A soul with no mate
So I will concentrate.

Jamie Baratt Winter (11)
South Milford School

A SEA OF FIRE

A stampede of butterflies
A dictionary of numbers
A sea of fire
A pillow of rock
A tiptoe of an elephant
A pencil case of apples
A book full of nothing
A reservoir of stones
A cup of giants
A cuddle of great white sharks.

Hayden Fitchett (10)
South Milford School

WEIRD

A pencil full of ink
A stampede of fish
A swimming pool of air
A pillow full of horns
An ice cube full of heat
A gang of no people

A fire full of snow
A mouthful of elephants
A shout full of whispers
A zoo full of humans
A book full of no pages.

Lloyd Harrison (11)
South Milford School

IF THE WALLS COULD TALK

They could tell how proud they were
They would sing with happiness
They would cry with terror
They would laugh when being built
They would freeze when Grendel came in
They would sing with joy
They would cry with sorrow
They would moan because of the bloodshed
In Hall Heorot.

Peter Denton (11)
South Milford School

A PATH FULL OF ROADS

A window of brick
A fire of ice
A pond of lead
A book of nothing

A sun of snow
A comedy of sorrows
A beach of paper
A soft toy of plastic

A swarm of sheep
A shed of concrete
A lemon of spice
A tiptoe of cows

A school of no one
A peace conference of wars
A pen of cardboard
A path full of roads.

Helen Twigg (10)
South Milford School

HALL HEOROT

If the walls could talk they would sing of joy
They would smile with pride
They would shudder from the cold
They would spy on Grendel
They would tremble for fear of Grendel
They would laugh from the jokes of the warriors
They would cry from the sadness of death.

Jonathan Booth (11)
South Milford School

KENNING - EMILY

Cartoon drawer
SATs dreader
Bed jumper
TV watcher

Ruler fiddler
Chair swinger
Raisin seller
Buddy helper

TV copier
PlayStation player
Comic reader
Music listener.

Emily Wilson (10)
South Milford School

A SWEET PINCH OF COFFEE

A class full of nobody
A careful group of rugby players
A herd of mice
A dry drop of rain
A tap full of nothing
A sweetness of coffee
A sour bag of sugar
A light drop of lightning.

Victoria Borradaile (11)
South Milford School

A DREAM FULL OF NOTHING

A window of brick
A weak bowl of jelly
A number line full of letters
A stampede of ballet dancers
A light bag of bricks
A book of glass
A dream full of nothing
A strong bolt of rain.

Katie Brittain (10)
South Milford School

THE UNKNOWN PARADISE

In the rainforest it is silent
And the rain from last night's monsoon has been swallowed up
By the green carpet on which tall trees rest their roots
The frothy water cascades over the mountainside
And parrots screech as they reach their nest
Tree frogs pounce on innocent bugs
And lap up cool water that has landed on moist leaves
During the rainy season.

As you head further into the rainforest
Brightly coloured petals flash past your eyes
Flowers and plants of all different types and sizes shoot through the soil
Chameleons rustle in the undergrowth
Fooling predators of what they are
And you feel like you're in a paradise no one has ever explored
It's unspoilt, it's perfect
Just like the world once was!

Sophie Dowlen (10)
Tranmere Park Primary School

THE SEA

The sea shimmers in sunlight,
Waves lap the shore,
Fish glide gently,
I couldn't want more.

Dolphins splashing and screeching,
Playing, having fun,
It glitters in the moonlight,
It sparkles in the sun.

There are white sandy beaches,
Coated with shells,
Children love to play there,
And breathe in the salty smells.

Seagulls hover around it,
Hunting for fish,
This is my dream holiday,
This is my wish.

Jemima Edwards (10)
Tranmere Park Primary School

The Beauty Of The Bird

Birds are beautiful in a weird sort of way,
They are brilliant colours, the brown thrush and the jay.
They chirp to each other and sing through the night,
Some fly as high as a bright soaring kite.

People will scare them, they are timid you see,
I just wish they weren't so scared, so frightened of me.
Magpies like shiny things like pennies and pounds,
But all of them are terrified of big, barking hounds.

They hunt food in the day, they feed their chicks in the nest,
When the day has flown by, they go back for a rest.
Their eggs can be speckled, their eggs can be sold,
Their eggs can be silver, or some pure gold.

Emily Shuttleworth (10)
Tranmere Park Primary School

Rock 'N' Roller Coasters

Twists, turns, loops and bumps,
Small ones, big ones
Nerve-breaking, throw up-making
Screaming, shouting, vomiting too

Take your pick, anywhere will do
Going nowhere, then have a load of fun
Parades, shows, rides too
They're all there for a bundle of fun

Fun-packed fairs
Stuffed-up stalls
Nerve-breaking, loopy loops
Finally, they all are the best.

William Tuff (10)
Tranmere Park Primary School

WHY MUMMY?

Why is the world so big Mummy?
Will it rumble in my tummy?
When did time begin?
Will it end in a dreadful sin?

Why Mummy, why?
Why are the clouds stuck in the sky?

Why do people stand and talk?
Why do people use a knife and fork?
Why do people go to school?
Why does it have to be a rule?

Why Mummy, why?
Why are clouds stuck in the sky?

Why do people drive in cars?
Why can't I live on Mars?
Why do I have to eat veg
And can I drive through a hedge?

No more questions Tommy!

Alexandria L Leighton (10)
Tranmere Park Primary School

SNOWY DAY

Snowflakes silently flutter from the sky,
Like silky white doves setting off to fly.
Icy ponds and frosty ground,
Brave little snowdrops struggle to be found.
Birds and hedgehogs hope to find something to eat,
A lonely worm would be a treat.

Children put on their gloves and hats,
While the cat sits snuggled on the mat.
Outside the children shout and play,
Wishing it could snow every day.
They all go sledging on the glittery hills,
Not bothering if they get the chills.

Snowballs flying everywhere,
Where they land they just don't care.
The hours go by, the snow is melting,
The heat of the snow is unrelenting.

Eleanor Henson (11)
Tranmere Park Primary School

MOONLIGHT

Moonlight enters the Earth below,
Its endless, illuminous, penetrating glow,
The shooting star plunges to the ground,
The speedy rocket twirls round and round.

The lonesome boy peers from his bed,
The UFO hovers overhead,
He releases the lock and opens the door,
There it is, the moonlight shimmering across the marble floor.

Ben Jones (11)
Tranmere Park Primary School

MY FANTASY WORLD

My fantasy world has chocolate covered mountains
And lemonade that runs down the fountains.

Where we sleep until lunchtime
And everything we say rhymes.

This is my world of chocolate fun,
This is my world where everything is yum.

School only lasts for four hours
And the pencils are made of flowers.

Where the homework's mostly drawing,
Because they think maths is boring!

This is my world of TV life,
This is my world where trees are as sharp as knives.

Where we can have friends over to sleep
And all the toys they let us keep.

Where children have their own houses,
And can have anything they want (even a mouse!)

This is my world where children rule.

Lucie Bennett (10)
Tranmere Park Primary School

THE RARE GIFT OF FRIENDSHIP

Friendship is a rare gift
That is born in everyone each day.
Very few people keep the gift in their hearts forever,
Some people lose it straight away.

When you lose a friendship,
It's like you've lost a twin.
When you gain a friendship
You'll never lose again.

Friendships are very fragile,
Very easily they break,
For if you want to keep them,
Be a friend with a heart at stake.

Friendships are like rainbows,
Each one special and unique.
Friendships are like sunsets,
Memories to keep.

Friendships are extraordinary,
Lost in their own world,
And that is why you'll always find
A true friend in this world.

Poppy Shuttleworth (10)
Tranmere Park Primary School

BLACKPOOL LIFE

I can hear relaxing, calm, peaceful, clear blue waves,
I can feel soft, warm, golden sand on my fluffy towel,
I can see a naughty, pinching, crab in the old, strong caves,
I can taste salty, bitter tastes on my tingling tongue,
I can smell salt and vinegar from the chips at the chip shop,
These are my senses on a beach at Blackpool.

I can hear screeching screams of the nervous people on the Pepsi Max,
I can feel a thrill rippling through my body,
I can see crashing dodgems as sparks fly from the rusting metals,
I can taste sticky, sickly, sweet candyfloss rotting my teeth,
I can smell pollution from the exhausts from the busy traffic,
These are my senses at the Pleasure Beach!

This is Blackpool life!

Emily Bell (10)
Tranmere Park Primary School

WINTER

When that one big shiver goes up your spine
And the wind goes through your hair
That shivery feeling in your arms
And that is the coldness in *winter.*

The sound of the cracking puddles
The solid grass crunching
The wind rustling in the trees
That is the sound of *winter.*

The sight of the cold snow
The bare trees stood all in a row
The fluffy flakes of snow falling from the sky
And that is the sight of *winter.*

Sophie Walker (8)
Wakefield Tutorial School

CHILDREN'S ALPHABET

A   is for apple all crunchy and sweet
B   is for banana all soft and tasty
C   is for cat all soft and black
D   is for dog so fast and cute
E   is for elephant so big and fat
F   is for fish all slippery and small
G   is for gorilla so noisy and crazy
H   is for hippopotamus all tough and hard
I   is for iguana all green amd scaly
J   is for jam all tasty and sweet
K   is for kitten so small and soft
L   is for lion so proud and bold
M   is for moon so big and bright
N   is for nurse so kind and good
O   is for octopus so soft and long
P   is for pig so dirty and pink
Q   is for queen so kind and sweet
R   is for rabbit all ears and smooth fur
S   is for slug so small and slimy
T   is for teacher so kind and nice
U   is for umbrella that keeps you dry
V   is for van to carry things about
W   is for window all transparent and white
X   is for X-ray to see some bones
Y   is for yo-yo so winding and round
Z   is for zebra so dangerous and fast.

Ajay Ramjas (8)
Wakefield Tutorial School

SCHOOL ORCHESTRA

Today is the concert for end of term,
Performed by the school orchestra.
Melissa and Tom play the clarinet,
And I play the flute and recorder.

During rehearsals I have practised well,
Blowing hard on my flute and recorder.
'You are much too quiet,' Mrs Tanner will say,
And then I blow even harder.

The orchestra meets at half-past six,
And we sit on the stage so high.
All the visitors fill the hall,
'Oh, why is my mouth so dry?'

Mrs Tanner smiles encouragingly,
As she taps her baton on her fingertips.
The audience waits expectantly,
As I raise my flute and purse my lips.

One more *toot toot* is all it takes,
To finish off the song.
This was my first time in the orchestra,
I'm glad it didn't go too wrong.

Philippa Varley (9)
Wakefield Tutorial School

SEASONS HAIKU

Crisp, smoky mornings
Shiny, red harvest apples
I love autumn days.

Crystal icicles
Snowflakes gently falling down
Swirling, whirling white.

Birdsong fills the air
Flowers bursting into life
Winter is over.

Lazy bumblebees
Sipping nectar here and there
Buzzing with pleasure.

Emma Reilly (10)
Wakefield Tutorial School

AUTUMN

Conkers, conkers here and there,
Conkers smashing, conkers bashing
Coloured leaves falling on the ground.

Leaves, leaves falling down from trees
Red, yellow, green and brown
On the trees falling down.

Animals are gathering here and there
Chestnuts, acorns and berries
For their winter feast.

Jessica Clegg (8)
Wakefield Tutorial School

There's A Mouse In The House

Oh dear, oh dear
My nan was filled with fear
It seems my nan had an unexpected guest
A peculiar one not like the rest.

She said she saw it under her bed
I said it was all in her head
Every day she would groan
'I can't sleep,' she would moan.

It got so bad
And nan was so sad
My mum said, 'Don't make such a fuss.'
But my nan said she needed to move in with us.

It was time to convince the mouse to move out
Because my nan wouldn't go home if there was any doubt.

We brought in a man with lots of traps
And the very next day
I'm pleased to say
The culprit was caught.

And once again, Nan is at home
Living alone!

Melissa Hirst (9)
Wakefield Tutorial School

THE RUBBISH ALPHABET

What's in the bin today? Look there is a . . .

A   vocado all rotten and black
B   aked beans all cold and runny
C   ottage pie all covered with potato
D   andelions all dead and shrivelled
E   clairs all the chocolate coming off
F   ish all smelly and rotten
G   rass all brown and muddy
H   ilda's mum's biscuits all soft and dull
I   ce cream all melted and lumpy
J   am all red and sticky
K   ebabs all burnt and black
L   ollipop sticks all bent and soggy
M   acaroni cheese all mouldy and smelly
N   ettles all stingy and green
O   nion skins all brown and smelly
P   ancakes all cold and yellow
Q   uilts all moth-eaten and dirty
R   adish all green and stringy
S   andwiches all white and stinky
T   arts all soft and sticky
U   mbrella all broken and turned out
V   inegar all strong-smelling and brown
W   alnut whip packet all chocolaty and wet
X   ylophone all dusty and broken
Y   oghurt pots all smelly and colourful
Z   ebra skin all dirty with no stripes.

Felicia Doubell (9)
Wakefield Tutorial School

MY FRIENDS ALPHABET

A   mair is my best friend
B   ob is cool
C   harles is big
D   aniel's good at dancing
E   ric is 10 years old
F   owler is a good football player
G   raham is a good pool player
H   eidi is my sister
I   an is my friend
J   essica is a girl
K   evin is a boy
L   ewis is my friend
M   artin is a diver
N   eville is a cleaner
O   wen is my brother
P   aul is my brother's friend
Q   uentin Blake is an author of a book
R   icky looks after me on Sunday
S   tuart Little is a TV star
T   ony is my dad's name
U   lrika is a TV presenter
V   iolet is a name of a flower
W   endy is from Peter Pan
X   is a secret
Y   olanda is in a story book
Z   ara is the queen's granddaughter.

Troy Anderson (8)
Wakefield Tutorial School

I CELEBRATE

I celebrate looking at my football trophy
That my team won.

I celebrate listening to the crowd
Cheering for our team.

I celebrate the smell of chocolate cake
It makes my tongue burn.

I celebrate the taste of oranges
They are sour and tongue-twisting.

I celebrate the feel of leather
It makes my hands cold.

I celebrate the memory . . .
When I won the football league.

Aamir Mayet (9)
Wakefield Tutorial School

FOOTBALLERS

Footballers are fit, fast and healthy,
If they are good they'll become wealthy.

There's Beckham and Owen, Gerard too,
Scholes and Smith, but that's only a few.

Golden Balls is Beckham, he shoots and then he scores,
All supporters cheer and applaud.

    England forever,
    Now altogether,
    We're on the ball!

Chris Lehan (10)
Wakefield Tutorial School

TEN LITTLE SNOWMEN

10 little snowmen sitting on a wall
One said he would jump it, but he didn't last at all.

9 little snowmen on a boat to Rome
One couldn't stand the sunlight and melted in the chair.

8 little snowmen sitting in the hall
One went to the toilet, couldn't get on and did it on the floor.

7 little snowmen flying back to home
One lost his snowball and couldn't find it at all.

6 little snowmen walking on the floor
One tripped and landed flat on the floor.

5 little snowmen running on a cliff
One tripped and fell off the cliff.

4 little snowmen setting rockets off
One held on and took off.

3 little snowmen lying on the floor
One was near the fire and melted through the floor.

2 little snowmen in their home
One went into the radiator and burnt himself out.

1 little snowman walking in a field
Tripped over a stick and landed under a wheel.

Sam Woodhead (8)
Wakefield Tutorial School

QUESTIONS AND ANSWERS

Where does the sky end?
Where the stars begin.
What are volcanoes?
Boils on the chest of Earth.
When will space collapse?
When the pillars of time fall.
What are countries?
The scabs on Mother Earth.
What are rivers?
God's tears rolling into the sea.
What comes after space?
Heaven and happiness.

Arran Fisher (11)
Weetwood Primary School

AFTERNOON

Afternoon ends with bell clanging
Afternoon ends with pencils flopping
Afternoon ends with coats zipping
Afternoon ends with Velcro ripping
Afternoon ends with feet pattering
Afternoon ends with clock ticking
Afternoon ends with me just listening
Afternoon ends and takes me home from school
Gentleman afternoon.

Jess Simmons (8)
Weetwood Primary School

CAT

Man sleeps
Cat weeps
Dog howls
Cat growls
Tiger roars
Cat snores
Leopard hides
Cat lies
Mouse squeaks
Cat creeps
Budgie flies
Cat dies.

Tess Furniss (10)
Weetwood Primary School

AFTERNOON

Afternoon ends with the computer beeping,
Afternoon ends with the doors screeching,
Afternoon ends with the pencils scraping,
Afternoon ends with the toilets flushing,
Afternoon ends with the chairs scratching,
Afternoon ends with the cups clanking,
Afternoon ends with me just listening,
Afternoon ends and takes me home from school.
Naughty Grandad afternoon.

Reece Cambridge Gray (7)
Weetwood Primary School

AFTERNOON ENDS

Afternoon ends
  With sharpening of pencils
Afternoon ends
  With the tutt-tutting of teachers
Afternoon ends
  With swishing of a paintbrush
Afternoon ends
  With the flicking of a book
Afternoon ends
  With quarrelling of children
Afternoon ends
  With splashing of tap water
Afternoon ends
  With me just listening
Afternoon ends
  And takes me home from school.
Smiling old woman afternoon.

Annie Lord *(7)*
Weetwood Primary School

GHOSTS

Ghosts come out at the midnight hour
Their howls and moans will make your lips go sour
They haunt and spook houses and people
They sometimes even go up to an old church steeple
Their bodies are a brilliant white
If you ever see one it will give you a fright
They come in all sorts of different shapes and sizes
And to frighten you even more they sometimes wear disguises
So readers beware, there are ghosts everywhere!

Elizabeth Roberts *(9)*
Weetwood Primary School

NIGHT

Night has a thin, dark dress, rippling,
Deep blue eyes staring
And pale lips whispering names.

Her tall figure drifting,
Moves nearer, calming,
A peaceful complexion, floating with the stars.

Pull up your cover,
Night will smother
And sleep will come.

Pure white moths fluttering,
Her dark woodland muttering,
Your thoughts drift away.

Within her calm countryside,
Her pitch-black horse gives you a ride.
Drink from her pure spring.

She appears so beautiful,
Ever meditating,
Shutting out all worries.

Night is healing,
Always dreaming,
Spirit, floating away.

Your breathing is slowing,
Rush of day is fading,
She sings you to sleep.

Holly Eyre (11)
Weetwood Primary School

QUESTION OF NATURE

What are mountains?
Dents of the Devil's club as he tries to
Escape from the centre of the Earth.

What are clouds?
The spirits of ancient giants.

What are trees?
Wise old men of nature.

Why do thunderstorms happen?
The demons at the centre of the Earth awaken.

What is space?
A dark meeting place for planets.

Where will lightning strike?
Where there is no light or hope.

What is language?
A way to explain Earth's mysteries.

John Hobley (11)
Weetwood Primary School

AFTERNOON

Afternoon ends with Velcro ripping.
Afternoon ends with coats zipping.
Afternoon ends with horns beeping.
Afternoon ends with patient humming.
Afternoon ends with car engines revving.
Afternoon ends with computer clicking.
Afternoon ends with me just listening.
Afternoon ends and takes me home from school.
Helpful Hobbit afternoon.

Joe Fogarty (7)
Weetwood Primary School

WINTER

She moves as a shadowy white cat,
Her misty grey eyes watching over the land,
She brings you into a frosty dimension,
Deadening all life with her icy fingers.

She drifts through her snow-covered world, alone,
Her tears fall as icicles in the
Trees of endless time
And hang as crystal twists on gnarled branches.

When autumn leaps away,
Her cloak trailing leaves,
She seizes the chance to dim the sun
And decorate the moon with frosty curls.

Some people fear her bewitching stare,
Her enchanting smile steals you away,
Beckoning to the place of
Eternal remembrance.

Can you hear?
Winter is near.

Beth Barker (11)
Weetwood Primary School

AFTERNOON

Afternoon ends with pupils whispering
Afternoon ends with feet banging
Afternoon ends with clock tick-ticking
Afternoon ends with Velcro r-r-ripping
Afternoon ends with chairs scraping
Afternoon ends with bell ting-a-linging.

Daniel Arundel (8)
Weetwood Primary School

WINTER

Cold and powerful, he stalks the Earth,
He's a tall, thin, ice-made man.
His trailing, frosty cape will smother all in its shadow,
He is winter.

Made of ice,
He can be kind, but
Do not upset him
For he controls the storms.

He whips up storms,
Which bring down snow.
He controls every blizzard,
All blinding snow and icy wind.

He carries his ice bow,
Bringing cold to all targets.
The arrows are made of glassy ice;
They carry winter frost.

Whispering and swirling,
Swooping over Earth,
He hovers over the frozen world,
Drifting everywhere.

His hair is sharp and pointy,
His eyes are dark and grey,
His mouth is cold and flaky,
His hands are gripping ice.

Cold and powerful, he stalks the Earth,
He's a tall, thin, ice-made man.
His trailing, frosty cape will smother all in its shadow;
He is *winter!*

Joseph Cresswell (11)
Weetwood Primary School

AFTERNOON

Afternoon ends with children chattering,
Afternoon ends with pupils giggling,
Afternoon ends with teachers shushing,
Afternoon ends with Velcro ripping,
Afternoon ends with kids feet skidding,
Afternoon ends with engines purring,
Afternoon ends with me just listening,
Gentle Granny afternoon.

Tom Emerton (8)
Weetwood Primary School

AFTERNOON

Afternoon ends with rubbers swishing
Afternoon ends with chairs clattering
Afternoon ends with clock ticking
Afternoon ends with children giggling
Afternoon ends with bodies swooshing
Afternoon ends with feet thudding, *thud*
Afternoon ends with me just listening
Afternoon ends and takes me home from school
Kind old lady afternoon.

Elinor Facer (8)
Weetwood Primary School

IN MY BOX . . .

(Based on 'Magic Box' by Kit Wright)

In my box . . .
I would put all the colours of the rainbow on the tail feathers of a bird.
The last laugh of my great grandmother,
The fizzy taste of sherbet on my tongue,
All the wild animals in the world,
All the happy faces smiling every day,
All the education in the world,
Yummy eggy bread sizzling in the frying pan,
The sweet scent of flowers,
My box is made of the brightest crystals in the world,
With smiles for hinges and the purest spirit to hold it all together
And the colours of the rainbow to bind it all together.

Aneesah Taylor (10)
Weetwood Primary School

TRAFFIC

Traffic is pink, blue and grey
It sounds like lions roaring all day
It smells like rubber burning
It makes me feel like my insides are churning
It tastes like a plastic wheel
It looks like a squirming eel.

Maya Kempe Stanners (8)
Weetwood Primary School

AFTERNOON

Afternoon ends with bell ting-a-linging
Afternoon ends with feet drumming
Afternoon ends with children chattering
Afternoon ends with teachers shushing
Afternoon ends with Velcro ripping
Afternoon ends with car engines purring
Afternoon ends with me just listening
Afternoon ends and takes me home from school
Thoughtful old Granny afternoon.

Elena Phylaktou (7)
Weetwood Primary School

AFTERNOON

Afternoon ends with paintbrushes swishing
Afternoon ends with pupils' pencils scratching
Afternoon ends with voices chattering
Afternoon ends with going home bell ringing
Afternoon ends with kids' coats zipping
Afternoon ends with children's feet drumming
Afternoon ends with me just listening
Afternoon ends and takes me home from school
Kind old Granny afternoon.

Mieke Armstrong (8)
Weetwood Primary School

AFTERNOON

Afternoon ends with bell squealing
Afternoon ends with children giggling
Afternoon ends with coats zipping
Afternoon ends with computers humming
Afternoon ends with lunch boxes banging
Afternoon ends with feet clattering
Afternoon ends with me just listening
Afternoon ends and takes me home from school
Kindness man afternoon.

James Letton (7)
Weetwood Primary School

AFTERNOON

Afternoon ends with lunch boxes banging
Afternoon ends with children giggling
Afternoon ends with computers humming
Afternoon ends with coats zipping
Afternoon ends with feet stomping
Afternoon ends with car engines spluttering
Afternoon ends with me just listening
Afternoon ends and takes me home from school
Graceful dear afternoon.

David Childs (7)
Weetwood Primary School

MY TWIN SISTER!

I have a twin sister, her name is Ellie May
She bosses me about every day.
I can't bear it,
She won't share it
And I wish she would do it my way.

I have a twin sister, her name is Ellie May
I always have to do what she does say.
When we play tig,
I have to dance a jig,
Oh please let it be my way.

Sophie Phylaktou (9)
Weetwood Primary School

AFTERNOON

Afternoon ends with bell tinkling
Afternoon ends with feet stamping
Afternoon ends with water bottles dripping
Afternoon ends with doors slamming
Afternoon ends with Velcro crackling
Afternoon ends with pencils squeaking
Afternoon ends with me just listening
Afternoon ends and takes me home from school.
Kind old lady afternoon.

Tom Simmons (8)
Weetwood Primary School

SKY, CLOUDS AND SEA

The sky is blue while clouds are white
Watching down on the joyful sight
They look to the left and look to the right
Trying not to get a big, big fright
At the astonishing great big sight
Down below on the left and the right
But where I am, where the sky is blue
And the clouds are white is just right
For me and the night or the height.

Calum Grant (8)
Weetwood Primary School

AFTERNOON

Afternoon ends with pupils chattering,
Afternoon ends with skirts swishing,
Afternoon ends with buckles tinging,
Afternoon ends with feet clattering,
Afternoon ends with coats zipping,
Afternoon ends with board pens squeaking,
Afternoon ends with me just listening,
Afternoon ends and takes me home from home.
Sweet old hedgehog afternoon.

Lydia Nelson (8)
Weetwood Primary School

AFTERNOON

Afternoon ends with paper swishing and rip-ripping
Afternoon ends with chairs scraping and scratching
Afternoon ends with feet tap-tapping
Afternoon ends with classroom shouting
Afternoon ends with coats swish-swishing
Afternoon ends with coats zip-zipping
Afternoon ends with me just listening
Afternoon ends and takes me home from school.
Gentle old woman afternoon.

Alex McFarlane (7)
Weetwood Primary School

AFTERNOON

Afternoon ends with the bell ring-ringing
Afternoon ends with children's feet drumming
Afternoon ends with kids' voices nattering
Afternoon ends with coats zipping
Afternoon ends with doors slamming
Afternoon ends with babies wailing
Afternoon ends with me just listening.
Soft Granny afternoon.

Rosie Paul (7)
Weetwood Primary School

AFTERNOON

Afternoon ends with sharpener scraping
Afternoon ends with paintbrushes swishing
Afternoon ends with blackboard chalk screeching
Afternoon ends with toilets gurgling
Afternoon ends with Velcro tearing
Afternoon ends with clock ticking
Afternoon ends with me just listening
Afternoon ends and takes me home from school.
Gentle elephant afternoon.

Merren Wallace (8)
Weetwood Primary School

AFTERNOON

Afternoon ends with pencils screeching
Afternoon ends with teachers' voices shushing
Afternoon ends with chairs scratching
Afternoon ends with children's voices giggling
Afternoon ends with feet stamping
Afternoon ends with rain pattering
Afternoon ends with me just listening
Kind old Granny afternoon.

Chloe Swan (7)
Weetwood Primary School

AFTERNOON

Afternoon ends with clock ticking
Afternoon ends with pencils tapping
Afternoon ends with chairs scratching
Afternoon ends with feet scraping
Afternoon ends with children screaming
Afternoon ends with doors slamming
Afternoon ends with me just listening
Afternoon ends and takes me home from school.

Lily McCann Tomlin (8)
Weetwood Primary School

AFTERNOON

Afternoon ends with rubbers squashing
Afternoon ends with pencils dropping
Afternoon ends with chairs scraping
Afternoon ends with water bottles splashing
Afternoon ends with feet clattering
Afternoon ends with doors slamming
Afternoon ends with me just listening
Afternoon ends and takes me home from school.
Lovely old woman afternoon.

Isobella Curtis (8)
Weetwood Primary School

WINTER

Slowly,
Hovering over Earth,
She waits . . .
Ready to pounce
And cast her evil upon us.
Still waiting . . .
Her eagerness builds up,
She is ready,
Ready to smother us,
With her cold heart and foul mind.

Her time has come,
She has already cast her
Immortal hatefulness upon the world,
Forceful and mighty,
With a foul mind.
Winter has everything you need
To rule the world.
For months and months
Winter
Can take over our lives,
Without our even knowing.

Ella Parker (10)
Weetwood Primary School

NIGHT

She stalks, she creeps,
Who could it be?
In a horrible dream
Who could put you under this curse?

She bites,
You scream,
You squeal
In your dream.

She makes you lost, lonely,
Who could it be?
Lurking in the shadows,
Impossible to see.

Her face, it is evil,
Her eyes spiteful,
Her black hair is strangled by knots,
Her fangs suck you into a sleep!

She hides away in the drawers at day,
Where the sheets are kept,
She is unseen, but heard,
Like the hiss of a cat.

You are in the safety of a stream at daytime,
But when night comes . . .
You are dragged - over, down a waterfall,
Crashing and falling, crashing and falling.

She tries to look beautiful
In a long evening dress;
But such a creature could not look pretty,
Not Night, Night, Night!

Becca Julier (10)
Weetwood Primary School

THE MAGIC BOX
(Based on 'Magic Box' by Kit Wright)

I will put in the box . . .
A silk, white tear on the first baby's cheek
The whales' song of secrets on a dark, silent night
The smell of fish and chips filling the air
And the seagulls crying above.

I will put in the box . . .
The first hold of a baby with a face so red
A cold, dark walk then a welcoming hot dinner
And the feeling of a mother's hug.

I will put in the box . . .
The wind blowing in my face
The soft, warm foam melting in my hand
And the sweet smell wafting round a rose.

I will put in the box . . .
A fairy wearing armour with sword and shield
A warrior skipping on light foot
And an elephant hugging a mouse.

My box is fashioned
From the stained glass windows of St Mary's Cathedral
And laced with the silk of a dragonfly's wing.
In each corner are bright beads shining like the morning sun.
My box is full of cushions of foam
And I would lie on them as the box flies through the clouds of mist.

Meg Barker (8)
Weetwood Primary School

AFTERNOON

Afternoon ends with teachers shushing
Afternoon ends with paintbrushes swishing
Afternoon ends with chairs screeching
Afternoon ends with bell squealing
Afternoon ends with lunch boxes colliding
Afternoon ends with children's feet drumming
Afternoon ends with me just listening
Afternoon ends and takes me home from school.
Soft Granny afternoon.

Courtney Taylor Browne (7)
Weetwood Primary School

AFTERNOON

Afternoon ends with lunch box trolley squealing
Afternoon ends with computers humming
Afternoon ends with cupboard door rumbling
Afternoon ends with football thudding
Afternoon ends with rubbers rubbing
Afternoon ends with bell screaming
Afternoon ends with me just listening
Afternoon ends and takes me home from school.
Helpful Hobbit afternoon.

Colvin Stokeld (7)
Weetwood Primary School

AFTERNOON

Afternoon ends with fish tank gurgling
Afternoon ends with pencils flicking
Afternoon ends with toilets flushing
Afternoon ends with bell ringing
Afternoon ends with Velcro zizzing
Afternoon ends with kids feet clattering
Afternoon ends with me just listening
Afternoon ends and takes me home from school.
Kind Nanna afternoon.

Natasha Lawes (7)
Weetwood Primary School

FEEDING THE FAMILY

Rats and mice, rats and mice,
When I feed it to my brother he says it's nice!

Corn and custard, corn and custard,
When I feed it to my sister she thinks of mustard!

Pizza and chips, pizza and chips,
When I feed it to my mummy it makes her sick!

Sophie Lancaster (8)
Weetwood Primary School

MY MAGIC BOX

(Based on 'Magic Box' by Kit Wright)

I will put in my box . . .
The first cry of a baby
The warmest summer we have ever had
The rustling of leaves on a dark night.

I will put in my box . . .
The beautiful smell of a joyful Christmas
The first day I saw my family
And the first word I ever said.

I will put in my box . . .
The funniest joke that someone ever said
A silky web covered in dewdrops
And the prettiest shell from a sixty-foot sandy beach.

I will put in my box . . .
A horse riding an elephant
A kangaroo driving a car
And a mouse playing catch with a lion.

My box is fashioned from tiny diamonds as precious as gold.
The lining is delicious Jelly Babies.

Hannah Taylor (8)
Weetwood Primary School

MY FAVOURITE TOY

Serenity is her name
She has sweeping white feathers and coal-black eyes
That twinkle in the night.
And when I go to bed
She stays by my side and sings
Keeping me from all harmful things.

Amelia Gwynne (9)
Weetwood Primary School

NIGHT

Night came to me at twilight,
A figure of worries, doom and despair,
Stalked so quietly, none could hear,
Whilst her hair flailed in curls and knots.

Night suddenly lurched towards me,
Clever as a cat.
Yet you still could not see her mysterious face,
As it was shielded by her dark, velvet hood.

Night then passed me,
As if scared to touch,
Yet I was sure I was still her unwilling victim,
As all the creatures in her path
Had fled far, far away.

Night breathed softly at me
And quickly turned the world I knew,
Into a dark, black mist,
Then a swirling void,
That sucked me into her world,
A world of nightmares, shadows and deep dwellings.

Nicola Bligh (11)
Weetwood Primary School

PLEASE DON'T . . . IT DOESN'T MATTER

Please don't judge me by my face,
By my religion or my race.
Please don't laugh at what I wear,
Or how I look or do my hair.
It doesn't matter if I lose or win,
It doesn't matter if I'm fat or slim.

Everyone is different, isn't that great?
We shouldn't decide who we love or hate.
We should all be treated exactly the same,
It doesn't matter if we're poor or have fame.

All I ask is to look inside
For the secrets I might hide.
I may not be pretty, I may not be tanned,
But if you look deeper, you'll see who I am.

Hanna Tuck (11)
Weetwood Primary School

FEEDING THE FAMILY

Breadcrumbs and cream, breadcrumbs and cream
When I feed it to my brother
It makes him scream.

Cabbage and fish, cabbage and fish
When I feed it to my mummy
She's sick in her dish.

Hot snail pie, hot snail pie
When I feed it to my daddy
It makes him die.

Tom Flockton (8)
Weetwood Primary School

NIGHT

I saw night
outside my window
last evening time,
I still remember her pale face
as white as the moon
and those eyes,
filled with stars;
you could see
the whole galaxy through them.
Her hair was wavy, like the ocean,
her mouth
the colour of the midnight sky.
She wore a long black cape
over her long draped dress;
she slightly hovered as she moved.
As soon as I saw her, many thoughts came
gushing into my head.

She looked kind
and calm, comforting,
but lonely,
lost in her own world,
waiting to come to Earth.
She may bring good dreams,
she may bring bad;
she's a burglar
stealing light
and day
and turning it into
darkness!

Stacey Saxton (11)
Weetwood Primary School

A POEM ABOUT NIGHT

Night is nasty because it's dark,
Night is nasty because it's scary,
Night is evil when it sparks,
Night is evil because it varies.

You think someone is going to get you at night,
Night is lonely because no one is with you.
If you wake up you will get a fright,
No one is there to save you!

Night is a burglar, who steals the light,
He takes all the good things from the day.
Be afraid, be very afraid of the night,
Because it will get you before you can shout, hey!

He has a scary face
His eyes are bloodshot red,
Watch out just in case
Otherwise you will be dead.

His mouth is big, bulgy and bold,
His hair is tatty and black,
He is horrible and cold,
So you might just want to watch your back.

He floats across the air
And lives in the middle of the Earth,
He is very mean and will scare
And hides under the earth.

Watch out for the fright,
Because it will get you in the middle of the night!

Robert Griffiths (10)
Weetwood Primary School

NIGHT

Night is a lady,
Who sweeps over the world.
Inside her sapphire necklace,
She holds the darkness.

Her long, sweeping dresses,
Are the colour of the moon.
And her green, curious eyes,
Have seen the end of space.

When daylight comes,
Lady of the night flees
To her distant home,
Quiet and undisturbed.

As she sleeps upon the moon,
Daylight will be in the world.
She is gentle and mild,
Loving and caring.

Night is a lady,
Who sweeps over the world.
Inside her sapphire necklace,
She holds the darkness.

Rebecca Mclaren (11)
Weetwood Primary School

THE MAGIC BOX
(Based on 'Magic Box' by Kit Wright)

I will put in my box . . .
The magic of a rainbow in a clear sky.
The beautiful, shiny horn of a silver unicorn.
The soft, silky whisper of the wind on a winter night.

I will put in my box . . .
The beauty of a sunset on a palm beach.
The fiery breath of the last dragon.
The first song of the lovely nightingale.

I will put in my box . . .
The summer sun on a stormy day.
A snowman riding a white horse.
The sandy rain falling one evening in spring.

I will put in my box . . .
The colourful wing of the beautiful dragonfly.
The delicate petals of the largest rose.
The gracefulness of the most gentle fairy.

My box is fashioned from light blue stained glass
The colour of the sky.
The fasteners would be icicles that could never melt
The top would be lined with silk the colour of grass.

Eilis Boyle (9)
Weetwood Primary School

THE MAGIC BOX
(Based on 'Magic Box' by Kit Wright)

I will put in my box . . .
A swift move of a horse's tail,
A flowing river moving along
And a coloured rainbow in the sky.

I will put in my box . . .
A tiny squeak of a timid guinea pig,
A magical world of the animals
And the sweet smell of melting chocolate.

I will put in my box . . .
A twinkling star in the sky,
A pink and purple sunset
And the clicking of a dolphin crying.

I will put in my box . . .
The sun in the middle of the night,
A hippo doing ballet
And a black summer.

My box is fashioned from
A purple, silky material,
With jewels around the edge
And a silver latch to open it.

Lucy Gorham (8)
Weetwood Primary School

MAGIC BOX
(Based on 'Magic Box' by Kit Wright)

I will put in my box . . .
The smell of cold autumn air.
A land of Dairy Milk chocolate.
The first smile of a baby.

I will put in my box . . .
A dolphin's song in a vast blue sea.
The first hug from my mum.
The feel of a crocodile's skin.

I will put in my box . . .
The brightest star of a moonlit sky.
The first slice of an Italian pepperoni pizza.
Stringy spaghetti covered in rich Bolognese sauce.

I will put in my box . . .
The 39th day of a summer month.
The nibble of a cheesy moon.
A flying pig in the air.

My box is fashioned from
Stained glass of a church
And the silk of a silkworm
It will be hinged with the sap of a tree.

Tom Laurence (9)
Weetwood Primary School

THE MAGIC BOX
(Based on 'Magic Box' by Kit Wright)

I will put in my box . . .
A wing of a butterfly
With wings as soft as a rabbit's fur.

In my box I will put . . .
Lots of birds singing
Their beautiful songs in the morning light.

My box is fashioned from
Everlasting wine gums
And chocolate buttons which taste so nice.

Zack Sikorski (8)
Weetwood Primary School

AFTERNOON

Afternoon ends with school bell squealing
Afternoon ends with teachers' voices shouting
Afternoon ends with magnets crashing
Afternoon ends with pencils scraping
Afternoon ends with car doors slamming
Afternoon ends with fire alarm screeching
Afternoon ends with me just listening
Afternoon ends and takes me home from school.
Kind old Grandad afternoon.

David Rodriguez-Saona (7)
Weetwood Primary School

FEEDING THE FAMILY

Fingernail pie, fingernail pie
When I feed it to my sister
It makes her cry.

Worms and peas, worms and peas
When I feed it to my mummy
It makes her sneeze.

Potato and cheese, potato and cheese
When I feed it to my dad
He lets out a scream.

Ben Humphris (9)
Weetwood Primary School

AFTERNOON

Afternoon ends with chairs screeching
Afternoon ends with shoes scraping
Afternoon ends with coats zipping
Afternoon ends with the bell br-br-bringing
Afternoon ends with doors swishing
Afternoon ends with me just listening
Afternoon ends and takes me home from school.
Oh helpful Herbert afternoon.

Jessica Harris (7)
Weetwood Primary School

MY MAGIC BOX

(Based on 'Magic Box' by Kit Wright)

I will put in my box . . .
A magic rainbow ride,
A song of the angels,
A falling, shining star.

I will put in my box . . .
An elegant pounce from a lion,
The wisp of the wind through my hair,
A snap of a twig under my foot.

I will put in my box . . .
A cat amongst the pigeons,
The first squeak of my mouse,
The first sip of my aunt Agevel's soup.

I will put in my box . . .
A sunbeam from the moon,
An everlasting rainbow,
A spider playing catch with a fly.

My box is fashioned from shell and rock,
The lining is the hardest scales of a dragon,
Inside is a world of fantasy and love.

Tina Walsh (8)
Weetwood Primary School

THE MAGIC BOX

(Based on 'Magic Box' by Kit Wright)

I will put in my box . . .
The twinkle of the first star in the night's sky,
The trickle sound of a sky-blue waterfall
And an icy snowflake falling from the sky.

I will put in my box . . .
A red and yellow sunset,
A hug from Mum and Dad
And the smell of fresh green grass.

I will put in my box . . .
A tiny screech of a small, brown mouse,
A small flap of a butterfly's wing
And a silent river flowing along.

I will put in my box . . .
A hamster flying an aeroplane,
A pig singing Christmas carols
And a cow riding a guinea pig.

My box is fashioned from pink and purple velvet
Gold, sparkly jewels and silver glitter round the edge.

Anna Morgan (8)
Weetwood Primary School

MY MAGIC BOX

(Based on 'Magic Box' by Kit Wright)

I will put in my box . . .
The first time I saw the glint in my mother's eyes
The cold touch of her hand
The first time I saw my family.

I will put in my box . . .
The love from my big brother
The first hug and the first word I said.

I will put in my box . . .
A sip of the clear blue waters of Spain
The last hug of my great, great uncle
A crystal from the most beautiful beach.

I will put in my box . . .
An elephant playing tig with a mouse
A cat and a mouse playing Monopoly
And a lion skipping and a hamster trying to drive.

My box is fashioned from Gold chocolate bar
Edged with chocolate red laces and stripes
And melted chocolate sprinkled on top.

Naomi Booth-Wade (8)
Weetwood Primary School

The Swakaknoca's Hullabaloo!

The Swakaknoca eats cherry trees,
It's as big as a lake and has knobbly knees,
Its pale white complexion reminds me of milk,
Its skin is so soft it shimmers like silk,
Its arms are rather short and stubby,
It has one eye and is rather tubby,
Slowly it advances with a wobble,
A bit of a lurch and sometimes a hobble,
Its breath has such a disgusting smell,
Wherever it's been you can certainly tell,
This creature is a gentle giant,
It has no friends but many a client,
You see it's surprising purpose is that,
It has an amazing ability to absorb fat,
All the creatures around you see,
Are now all fit and healthy,
All around the world rejoice,
The Swakaknoca's just won the people's choice,
A celebrity style party was planned,
With cherry tree puddings and a big brass band,
To witness this beast dancing and singing,
Was a spectacle truly worth seeing,
The ground shook and landscapes shifted
And everybody's spirits were lifted,
By far the best of any do,
    The Swakaknoca's hullabaloo!

Dominic Lowe (11)
West End Primary School

HULLABALOO!

There's a pie in the sky that flies so high
Higher than you or me
It goes round the world
At a million miles an hour
And never lands under a spitting shower.

There's a pie in the sky that flies so high
Higher than you or me
It dodges people black and white
And likes to see cows during flight.

There's a pie in the sky that flies so high
Higher than you or me
It goes to see Teletubbies, Fimbles and Tweenies
And hates to see horrible meanies.

There's a pie in the sky that flies so high
Higher than you or me
It went to a party *Hullabaloo!*
The wine was drunk, the eggs got beaten
Oh no, I've been eaten!

Ryan Clarkson
West End Primary School

HULLABALOO

You think that all we do in the day
Is swim around in the sea and play
But our life isn't as easy as you've been told
Me and my friends often get cold.

We wobble and waddle on our feet
And we dive to catch our fish to eat.

We have to walk on the snowy-cold ground
So we huddle together in big, warm crowds
We can't play in the icy-cold sea
Even the other penguins agree.

We lie in the soft, fluffy snow
Which is very cold as you should know
Hullabaloo what can we do,
We can't keep on living like this, could you?

Rachel Borkala (10)
West End Primary School

HULLABALOO!

The reluctant duvet shivers
As it falls off the high, warm bed
The snotty alarm sneezes and sniffles
And blows its trumpet to wake the sleeping log.
As I walk the light opens its bright eyes to stare at me,
The snoozing stairs snore as I creep
My Coco Pops crackle as I pour the ice-cold milk
Then I run towards the door and leave the house.

Rebecca Hutchinson (11)
West End Primary School

HULLABALOO

Hullabaloo, what shall I do?
Hullabaloo, I don't know what to do.
So many questions, so little time
Hullabaloo, what shall I do?

The clock is awake as the time flies by
The sound of pencils scratching, there's so little time,
Here comes the next question
I don't know what to do!

Is it right, is it wrong?
Hullabaloo, what shall I do?
The time is up but is it right or is it wrong?
In my head words spin around, it's gone blank what can I do?
My lips are sealed, I don't know what to say,
There is a question somewhere in my head,
Hullabaloo, what can I do?
There's an answer somewhere, but where?
Hullabaloo!

Benita Guest (10)
West End Primary School

HULLABALOO

The reluctant duvet shivers as it falls off the high, warm bed
The snotty alarm sneezes and sniffles
And blows its trumpet to wake the sleeping logs.
Light flickers once or twice before it gleams down at me
The screeching stars scream as a herd of elephants slide down
Crunchy monsters swim for their lives in the white sea
Finally I lure the bag onto my back.

Ashley Miller (11)
West End Primary School

HULLABALOO

The owl sits steadily on his perch,
His huge, yellow eyes gleam in the darkness,
He is listening to the world around him,
He knows the night world.

In the bushes far below a mouse scurries along,
To the owl this sounds like a giant stamping,
He lifts his wings to catch the mouse,
This is food for him.

The grass rustles in the wind,
To the owl this sounds like an aeroplane starting up,
Humans far in the distance shout and cry,
This annoys the owl, he shuffles his feathers and blinks his eyes.

A cricket croaks in the undergrowth,
To the owl this sounds like an out of tune violin,
Another owl flies past and stares at the owl,
He stares back.

To the owl everything is a hullabaloo,
He knows everything, but he does not let it show,
The owl can never properly be asleep.

Caroline Poulter (11)
West End Primary School

HULLABALOO!

There are so many animals in the world,
I see and see again,
I'd love to see a green hippo again and again.
And so I see a green hippo wandering by,
He sees me again and again,
Wandering through my mind.
And one day I see him for real,
Wandering down the street,
I ask myself, is he real?
And he went by and asked me,
'Are you real sir or are you just pretend?
I hope you are real sir, or else we can be friends.'
He asks me, 'Is this street always a hullabaloo?
Or now we can be friends.'

Laura Mallinson (10)
West End Primary School

HULLABALOO

Guests pass through the gates with amazement
They stare into the neon lights as they pulsate in an angry way
Roller coasters rush down the brightly coloured tracks
At eye-boggling speeds
Merry-go-rounds whirl out of control
To the delight of the whizzing guests.
Ferris wheels stand tall above the rowdy crowd
The multicoloured train races down to the station with its glowing eyes
Guests rush past the chip stands, paying little attention
To the shouting offer banners
The ghost train speeds upwards with a scream to the broken window
Screams fill the air. Hullabaloo.

James McKenzie (10) & Michael Ambler (11)
West End Primary School

HULLABALOO

The hullabaloo on the street,
The hustle and bustle, the loud noises,
The gossip of lives, swarming like bees through the cold air.

A homeless person lives on the street,
Knows a few things,
He knows that Sally is pregnant,
He knows that Mr and Mrs Jones are divorcing,
In fact he knew before Mr Jones.
The roar of traffic fills his ears, the smoke and fumes make him cough,
But still no one notices him - to the people around him he is nothing,
To them he's invisible, not there.
He still has a mind, a pair of ears
And can still listen to the lives around him.
He knows that Ben is meeting Michelle at 8,
Ben mentioned it on his mobile.
An argument took place on Becky's phone
Something about being jealous.

The hullabaloo on the street,
The hustle and bustle, loud noises,
The gossip of lives, swarming like bees through the cold air.

Lizzy McCarthy (10)
West End Primary School

HULLABALOO

My cat Tom is a cat like no other cat
All day he will be asleep
All night the coolest cat around
He will go and play in the town
The town would suddenly light up
To greet him in a powerful way
He'd call on all his friends
They would meet up at the town hall
Gingers and whites, tabbies and alley cats
They would break into the fish shop next door
But then it would begin to snow
And silly cats would run for home
While Tom would decide to go sledding
They'd slip and slide up and down
Thinking children would never dare do this
But when the snow came too deep
Tom would head for the trees
To sit and wait for day
Then when the morning came
He would frown and complain
Tom would then run and catch the 42 bus
Just to get home to me!

Katie Farrar (10)
West End Primary School

HULLABALOO

The stubby monster in my room,
Likes to hide in the gloom.
He'll come out with only me,
But when someone comes, he'll hide swiftly.
When he hears a whisper he'll crouch down
Under the bed without a sound.
He'll turn invisible like a shot
And hide in the darkest, messiest spot.
He hates the light, he'll never come out,
At least not while the sun's about.
The only time he'll come out,
Is when it's raining lightly down.
The tempestuous weather makes him hide
He'll burrow deep inside his dustbin under the bed
Using his arms to cover his head
My mum found him out yesterday afternoon
It's gonna be a hullabaloo!

Daniel Barron (11) & Alistair McKenzie (10)
West End Primary School

HULLABALOO

The duvet creeps to stay warm as I shiver
Curtains hiss as I slowly draw them back
The shower tries to wake me up with its loud, crackly hiss
The little scrubbing brush squeaks as it washes my teeth
The stairs squeal as I creep down to breakfast
As I feed my school bag with school books it makes a loud
                                        chomping noise

What can I do? Hullabaloo.

Cassandra Helen Quarmby (11)
West End Primary School

HULLABALOO!

In the world we have
Pollution and fumes in the air,
Drought and floods,
Sometimes it feels
Like Mother Nature doesn't care,
Flowers, pretty and bright,
And the twinkling stars that shine at night,
Endangered animals' hopes are lost,
We must protect them at all costs,
Trees stand tall and proud,
Their branches tingle as they try to touch the clouds,
The community of people on Earth,
Work together to witness technology's birth,
Our memories stand clear in our minds,
We remember all our precious finds,
What we see now
May change what happens in the future,
The world needs our help!

Natalie Falls (11)
West End Primary School

HULLABALOO!

The wind blows a cool breeze
across the shining meadows,
as it swirls round, round and back again.
The sun smiles down on the scene
as her hot gaze shines over the world.

Suddenly the thunder wakes from his sleep,
sending deep dark clouds
to blot out the brightness of the sun.

The lightning strikes the wind
and with swirls it fades away.
The meadows that used to shimmer to and fro
now lay flat from the pelting of rain.
The trees shiver
with shadows that fall across them
and all birds' nests lay empty.

The days pass by like a clock ticking,
day has become night!

Rebeccah Yeadon (10)
West End Primary School

HULLABALOO

He lies along the coral reef,
Slow lungfish wriggle beneath.
The sun parches his smooth, round back,
A life of movement is what he lacks.
He sees all the dolphins and massive blue whales,
Very small yachts and huge ships' sails.
All whirlpools make a horrible noise,
As they whip up ships and cabin boys.
He's seen all the ages of pirates and sailors,
Children dashing with ice cream and wafers.
Volcanoes burst, erupt and clatter,
Old ghost ships drift down and shatter.
Little sea snails pick at sharks' bones,
Other rocks argue in grunts and moans.
At the coast is where waves break,
A seal dives down and eats a sea snake.
As the night draws on he knows not what to do,
A little stone in a hullabaloo!

Benjamin Vickers (11)
West End Primary School

HULLABALOO

Hullabaloo the town is crazy,
dustbins sneezing and letter boxes screaming and shouting,
casinos heaving with crazy teenagers,
flats are sleeping, shops and offices close their mouths,
the nightclubs are dancing away,
the trees are having a great time,
the rattling of the money wasting away,
rats are eating all the dump,
nobody realises what's going on,
flashing, flickering street eyes are going mental,
children are crying for their parents to come home,
teenagers are throwing eggs and snowballs at the school property,
the babysitters can't control the kids,
teachers are trying to study against the noise.

William Leung (10) & Matthew Wilkinson (11)
West End Primary School

HULLABALOO!

A very good footballer named Mark Viduka,
Came from Australia and liked to play snooker.
Scored 10 goals by half-past nine,
But got sent off before half-time,
His head hung in shame,
And he could not finish the game,
He walked through the tunnel with everybody booing,
The manager knew for a fact he had to start suing,
He hung up his boots and he's off like a shot,
He goes to the shower and puts it on hot,
He gets out of the shower and turns off the power,
Steps in the car and drives very far.

Conor Lowson & Jordan McKenna (10)
West End Primary School

SING, HULLABALOO, SING

My teacher, she drives me crazy
She never stops singing
She thinks she's good, but she's 100% not
She sings my best mate's poems
She laughs at things that are not funny
But don't get me wrong
She's good looking, kind and seriously funny
But really does she have to sing?
What makes her sing?
Is it the fresh smelling flowers
Or the green, green grass?
Whatever it is, it drives me crazy!
She never sings in summer
It's always in winter
I suppose she's crazy
Well that makes two of us
Hullabaloo, what can I do?

Corie Megan Jackson (10)
West End Primary School

HULLABALOO

When I was put in a new class
With different people all over,
I was split up from my best friend.
The teacher told everyone
To get into partners
And do the work together.
I looked all around
Wondering who to go with.
A girl walked over,
The same look on her face,
Her eyes flashed at me.

In the playground
I looked all over
For the girl
I had thought about
Non-stop.
I walked hither and thither,
Back to front,
When luckily I found her
Playing basketball.

I asked her if
I could sit next to her at lunch.
But when she said
She was sitting next to her best friend
My eyes started to water.
I asked who she was,
A girl walked over,
Her hair in a bun,
I thought to myself,
Maybe she's better.

Lauren Cooke (11)
West End Primary School

HULLABALOO

My cat's gone crazy, hullabaloo
I really don't know what to do
It swings on the light
Makes it look like night
Hullabaloo, what can I do?

Aliens in hammocks
Causing havoc
Bright lights flashing
Gozumpas dashing
A barmy army of illiterate ants
Carrying socks and underpants
Hullabaloo, what can I do?

Golfers putting
Head teachers running
A psycho sprout
Butchering a trout
Hullabaloo, just what can I do?

Marmalade monsters in the night
Designed to give a super fright
The sky turned green and out came the queen
On anti-gravity boots
Hullabaloo, what can I do?

The wicked spirit of Azkaban
Is learning to drive a hot dog van
Hullabaloo, what can I do? Maybe something later.

Alex Postle (11)
West End Primary School

HULLABALOO

How far a penny can travel,
Through the sewers and onto the gravel,
Passed on by sweaty palms,
Pulled out of pockets and put into see-through jars,
Put in banks to save for the future,
Pennies are given to pay for the tutor,
Laying on the floor covered up,
The penny gives off a sparkling look,
And attracts the eye to pick it up.
Oh what luck.
Some call this a lucky penny as valuable as gold,
But it may be as black as it is cold.

The pennies are swapped and exchanged for food,
The change is given, one penny or two?
A tramp walks by begging for money,
He asks for a penny but I gave him too many.

Alex Fitch & Jake Woodward (10)
West End Primary School